TEENS ~ BODY IMAGE AND BEYOND

Facilitator Reproducible
Activities for Groups
and Individuals

Ester R.A. Leutenberg

Carol Butler, MS Ed, RN, C

Illustrated by
Amy L. Brodsky, LISW-S

Duluth, Minnesota

Whole Person
101 West 2nd St., Suite 203
Duluth, MN 55802

800-247-6789

books@wholeperson.com
www.wholeperson.com

Teens – Body Image and Beyond
Facilitator Reproducible Activities for Groups and Individuals

Copyright ©2013 by Ester R.A. Leutenberg and Carol Butler. All rights reserved. Except for short excerpts for review purposes and materials in the activities and handouts sections, no part of this book may be reproduced or transmitted in any form by any means, electronic or mechanical without permission in writing from the publisher. Activities and handouts are meant to be photocopied.

All efforts have been made to ensure accuracy of the information contained in this book as of the date published. The author(s) and the publisher expressly disclaim responsibility for any adverse effects arising from the use or application of the information contained herein.

Printed in the United States of America

10 9 8 7 6 5 4 3 2 1

Editorial Director: Carlene Sippola
Art Director: Joy Morgan Dey

Library of Congress Control Number: 2013936471
ISBN: 978-157025-301-0

Dedication

I dedicate this book to...

our children, Mitchell, Kathy, Lynne and Amy who originally taught me how to be a mom of teenagers

and our grandchildren, Sophia, Nick, Ari, Jenny, Mason; Moselle, Avi, Shai; Kyle, Tyler and Evan, who continue my education!

Ester Leutenberg

I dedicate this book to...

my daughter, Tambria whose adolescent challenges helped her become the person and counselor she is today

and my granddaughter Amber who emerged from her teens a wonderful woman and mother; and my granddaughter Myriah whose teen years are yet to come.

Carol Butler

Deepest Gratitude

Our gratitude to these teen counselors for their input...

Annette Damien, MS, PPS
Beth Jennings, CTEC Counselor

And to these teens for their insights...

Joseph Dritch
Hannah Lavoie
Moselle Yulish

And to these professionals who make us look good!

Art Director – Joy Dey
Editor and Lifelong Teacher – Eileen Regen
Editorial Director – Carlene Sippola
Illustrator – Amy L. Brodsky
Proofreader – Jay Leutenberg

Purpose of the Book, Teens – *Body Image and Beyond*

Body image affects males and females; puberty's physical changes, combined with identity, popularity, and athletic pressures, contribute to adolescent challenges. Food and weight are not the only issues; preoccupation with facial features, skin, hair, clothes and height, and striving for brawny builds or hourglass figures undermine peace of mind and divert attention from other aspects of self and life.

Teens – Body Image and Beyond helps teens to accept their body types and inherited features, see differences as distinctions, and know their appearance is not their identity.

Media messages, online profiles, friends, sports, eating disorders, muscle madness, temptations to use steroids or diet pills, and other issues are addressed. Teens will be encouraged to value variety in shapes and sizes and to embrace their own and others' uniqueness.

Young people who wish to change alterable traits will receive nutrition and fitness tips. Teens with gender identity concerns will know that they are not alone and they will learn how to access professional expertise.

Dating is laden with body image issues; teens will consider whether they pursue partner-pressured perfection or are self-directed. Teens will identify the non-physical appeal and qualities they seek in partners and relationships.

While the intensity of body image challenges is validated, teens will be encouraged to build character, ponder ethical dilemmas, see struggles as steppingstones, and find ways to be charitable.

Adolescent Appeal is Essential

Teens like to be active and interact; games, role plays, panel discussions and team activities promote movement and fun; thought-provoking questions encourage verbal and artistic expression; teens create posters, poetry, slogans and skits; they play expert advisors to each other.

Teens who prefer private self-examination are equally served; facilitators who believe their teens need introspection rather than interaction have that option; most sessions are adaptable for individual or group activities.

Launching Life

Identities developed during adolescence set the stage for life. Keeping physical appearance in perspective and prioritizing internal attributes helps teens forge ahead as whole persons whose heads, hearts and hands mean more than faces and figures.

Out of the mouths of babes oft times come gems; teens, older and wiser than babes, are able to learn, grow, discern truths, develop values and influence peers with *pearls of wisdom*.

For the Facilitator Using Teens – *Body Image and Beyond*

FORMAT

An Introduction for Participants to motivate teens for the activities (Page 7).

A chapter cover sheet with a related quotation and a description of each session.

Ten chapters, two to nine sessions per chapter . . .

- My Profile
- My Friends
- My Genes and My Genes
- Shape, Size and Sports
- A Different Perspective
- Body Size Diversity
- Are You What You Eat?
- Work Out or Play?
- Sexual Image
- Beyond Body

Reproducible page(s) for each session – most are adaptable to individual or group activities.

Each session supplies an explanation *For the Facilitator* which includes:

  I. Purpose – goals for the teens

  II. General Comments – brief background information

  III. Possible Activities – ways to introduce the topic; interactive and/or individual activities

  IV. Enrichment Activities – additional learning opportunities

Most activities provide more than enough material for a **fifty minute group or individual session**; if more time is needed, facilitators may wish to assign homework or continue topics at the next meeting.

Delicate issues are addressed; **facilitator discretion is advised**. Feel free to photocopy a page, white out text and/or write in additional information, then reproduce and distribute.

Facilitators are reminded to **refer troubled teens** for a psychiatric evaluation if they appear severely depressed, admit to thoughts about harming themselves or others, have been or are being abused, or based on your intuition, indicate they need more help. Follow all legal reporting requirements. If threats are imminent, call 911 or local emergency numbers.

Teens need to know that **keeping secrets can kill**. If they are aware that a peer wants to harm self or others, they need to tell a trusted adult. Breaking a confidence to save lives is honorable.

Tips for Presenting This Information to Teens

> ***To know how to suggest is the great art of teaching.***
> ~ Henri Frederic Amiel

Ask, don't tell, whenever possible.

Teens learn by doing; active involvement versus passive listening has greater impact.

Working in teams or pairs makes most sessions more enjoyable.

Encourage a teen to list peers' ideas on the board during brainstorming.

Allow teens to ponder problems and possible solutions and arrive at their own conclusions.

Encourage teens to respectfully disagree during the many opportunities for discussion and debate.

Encourage disclosure at each individual's comfort level.

To encourage personalized modes of expression, opportunities for talking, role plays, games, drawing and writing are provided. Allow teens to deviate from the suggested activities to use any safe method to communicate.

Remind teens to share what is true for them; there are few right or wrong answers.

Ask teens to pour feelings onto paper without censorship; mechanics, spelling or artistic ability are unimportant in these instances.

Remind teens to use code names so that only the writer knows the person's identity. Example: if their friend Greg loves baseball, use *HLB for He Loves Baseball* when referring to him.

Although an agenda is provided, deviate at will! You know your teens, what they need, what will work.

If a topic of high interest and relevance emerges, seize the moment; return to your plan later or tomorrow!

Encourage teens to talk privately with you after a group session if overwhelming emotions or issues surface; remind them that additional professional help and support groups are available; refer and report abuse or threats as warranted.

Teens – *Body Image and Beyond*
Introduction for Participants

Body image is big!

It affects your identity, popularity, dating, athletics, employment, and your life.

Some aspects of appearance can be changed; some cannot.

Your can alter your image and its importance.

Despite media madness and pressures for perfection, you have the power to change your perspective and make peace with your uniqueness.

You may decide that your head, hands, and heart matter more than your face and form.

You can develop and cherish internal aspects of your identity.

As you complete the handouts, or participate in activities, consider the following:

- Think for yourself, give honest opinions, express feelings, ask questions.
- Respond thoughtfully; write for you, yourself, not for class or publication; draw for your eyes only, unless you wish to share.
- If overwhelming emotions arise, ask for one-to-one time with your teacher or counselor; tell a parent or care provider.
- If a peer tells you about wanting to harm self or others, tell a trusted adult. Secrets kill; sharing saves lives! If there is no one to tell, call 911 or your local emergency services number.
- Any person in emotional distress may go to a hospital emergency room for help.

You will have opportunities to discuss, debate, advise peers, and make decisions. Ultimately, you decide the value you place on looks; what you love; how you live.

> **We don't receive wisdom;
> we must discover it for ourselves,
> after a journey no one can take for us or spare us.**
>
> ~Marcel Proust

Teens – *Body Image and Beyond*

TABLE OF CONTENTS

1. MY PROFILE 11
- InSight 13
- Dear Advice Columnist 15
- Body Bias BINGO 17
- I-Messages 19
- Coin a Phrase 21

2. MY FRIENDS 23
- Bigger Than 25
- My Solar System 27
- Staying Power 29
- Friends Don't Squelch or Squash 31

3. MY GENES AND MY JEANS 33
- Morphs that Don't 35
- Trait-agories 37

4. SHAPE, SIZE AND SPORTS 39
- Shapes and Sports 41
- Steer Away: Steroids and Male Athletes 43
- Pain and No Gain: Steroids and Female Athletes 45
- Mirrors and Muscles 47
- What is Sportsmanship? 49

5. A DIFFERENT PERSPECTIVE 51
- What's My Secret? 53
- Who Is On My Team? 55
- Emotional Overeating: Are you a Tortoise or a Hare? .. 57
- Scratch the Surface 59
- Ace the Quiz 61
- Cut Out Cutting 63
- Disarm Disability 65

6. BODY SIZE DIVERSITY ... 67
- Weight: War and Peace ... 69
- Spin to Win ... 71
- Size and Sensitivity ... 73
- Body Topics for Blogs and/or Panels ... 75–77

7. ARE YOU WHAT YOU EAT? ... 79
- Agree? or Disagree? ... 81
- Habits Make Us ... 83
- Starve, Stuff or Solve? ... 85
- Create Your Own ... 87
- Food Fact Jeopardy ... 89

8. WORK OUT OR PLAY? ... 91
- Pics and Tips ... 93
- A - Z Fitness ... 95
- Price Fair ... 97

9. SEXUAL IMAGE ... 99
- Transbodies ... 101
- Puppet? Marionette? Your Own Person? ... 103
- Magnetism ... 105

10. BEYOND BODY ... 107
- Body Idioms Art and Reflections ... 109
- Charades ... 111
- Blinders: On or Off? ... 113
- What's Eating You? ... 115
- Character Clues ... 117
- Pro and Con ... 119–121
- Self-Centered or Not in Vain? ... 123
- Never Say Never! ... 125
- Silent Heroes ... 127

INTERNET RESOURCES ... 129

MY PROFILE 1

Attitude is more important than the past, than education, than money, than circumstances, than what people do or say. It is more important than appearance, giftedness, or skill.
— CHARLES R. SWINDOLL

InSight .... page 13 ▶
Teens lose their sight momentarily; then open eyes, and minds, to society's unrealistic standards, media madness and peer pressure regarding appearance.

Dear Advice Columnist ... . page 15 ▶
Teens role-play advice columnists, answering fictitious letters about looks, dating, popularity and other issues; additionally, teens may compose anonymous real-life problem letters and receive peer feedback.

BODY BIAS BINGO .... page 17 ▶
Teens play BINGO and consider cultural bias, advertising agendas and role models; celebrities with talent and humanitarianism are compared to those with superficial appeal.

I-Messages .... page 19 ▶
Teens liken self-talk to electronic messages by deleting negative thoughts, replacing them with positive but realistic I-messages and noting resultant changes in feelings and actions.

Coin a Phrase .... page 21 ▶
Through a coin-toss game, teens analyze and personalize quotations about enduring aspects of profiles or personhood.

My Profile ▶

InSight

ONLINE PROFILE

UNREALISTIC STANDARDS

MEDIA BIAS

MEDIA LITERACY

OBSESSION

EMACIATED MODELS

COMPARISON

COMPETITION

AUTHENTIC

FAVORITISM

POPULARITY

STEREOTYPES

SOCIAL HIERARCHY

PERSPECTIVE

TOUCH-UP

WEIGHT NEUTRALITY

ROLE MODELS

EMOTIONAL IMMUNITY

RUBENESQUE

UNCONDITIONAL ACCEPTANCE

UNIQUE

EXTERNAL MOTIVATION

INTERNAL MOTIVATION

TEENS – Body Image and Beyond

InSight
FOR THE FACILITATOR

I. Purpose
   To boost awareness of media madness and stereotypes dictating what's cool and how teens *should* look.

II. General Comments
   Teens live in a material world; this helps teens replace probable prior unawareness with insight.

III. Possible Activities

   1. Individual Activity

   Distribute the *InSight* handout and ask teens to define and apply some of the terms to their experiences in writing and/or aloud.

   2. Blindfold Game
   a. Before session write the terms on the board, scattered randomly, as on the handout.
   b. Tell teens they will be blindfolded, then able to see and gain insight about the terms.
   c. Teens take turns holding one hand over their closed eyes, and pointing the other index finger forward. (A blindfold may be used if preferred).
   d. A volunteer guide accompanies each contestant to the board, to ensure safety.
   e. The blindfolded teen touches the board with an index finger and opens his/her eyes.
   f. The teen defines the term closest to his/her finger and applies it to personal experience, and/or asks for peer ideas; no one is put *on the spot!* Erase terms as they are used.

Elicit the following concepts:

Online profile – Teens put their best face forward in photos, attract friends, appear cool.
Unrealistic standards – Society expects muscle men, hourglass females, symmetrical faces.
Media bias – TV, movies, music videos and magazines promote thinness or machismo.
Media literacy – Awareness of sex appeal in ads promising perfection through products.
Obsession – Fixation on popularity, appearance; focusing excessively on a perceived flaw.
Favoritism – Preference or prejudice in jobs, popularity, etc., based on appearance.
Emaciated models – The former standard; current efforts are to promote healthier looks.
Comparison – Looking at self in relation to a fashion model or weight-lifter.
Touch-up – Processes done to photos to make celebrities look better.
Competition – Trying to have the best body, the most friends, the coolest clothes.
Authentic – Being the real you, not trying to impress others or achieve popularity.
Popularity – Status and recognition usually due to looks, athletic prowess, or clothing.
Stereotypes – Discrimination against differences; how cool people *should* look, dress, act.
Unique – Valuing individuality; seeing a difference as a positive distinction.
Social hierarchy – False status of a clique; the haves and have-nots; in-groups and outcasts.
Perspective – Viewing character as more important than appearance, cars, performance.
Weight neutrality – Not chasing a perfect weight; focusing on what really matters to you.
Emotional Immunity – Ignoring toxic comments, knowing the truth about your attributes.
Role models – Rock stars, celebrities, athletes; Barbie and Ken; people who use their fame to promote humanitarian efforts; people in science, politics, the arts, etc. who improve the world.
Rubenesque – Rubens painted sensual, full-bodied women; plumpness was pleasing!
Unconditional acceptance – Love of self and others regardless of face, figure, fashion.
External motivation – Looking or acting to please others, for applause or approval.
Internal motivation – Desire to be kind, competent, etc., for inner rewards.

IV. Enrichment Activity
   Encourage teens to discuss, *Everything has its beauty, but not everyone sees it.* ~ **Confucius**

My Profile

Dear Advice Columnist …

1 My partner always stares at people with better bodies than mine. I feel inferior. What can I do?	**2** I'm a thin male with good grades. How do I find a girlfriend?	**3** People are bullying and bad-mouthing me online and in person. What can I do?	**4** I'm thinking about diet pills to be thin so people will want to go out with me. How will this work?	**5** My friend always borrows my clothes. Does she like me or my clothes? What should I do?
6 My parents constantly complain about my appearance. What can I do?	**7** I'm a plain female who males call a friend. How do I find romance?	**8** My friends laugh at different ethnic groups. What can I do?	**9** I'm thinking about steroids to be better in sports. What do you think?	**10** Females flock to jocks. I'm good at art but terrible in sports. How do I find a girlfriend?
11 I am jealous of good looking, popular people. What can I do?	**12** Better looking people are trying to steal my partner. What can I do?	**13** My parents disapprove of my friends based on their looks. What can I do?	**14** I plan to use drugs so I can lose weight. What do you think about this idea?	**15** I want to be in the popular clique but I don't look or act cool. What can I do?
16 I can't afford the trendy clothes most people wear. What can I do to be accepted?	**17** People are jealous of my great face and perfect body. How do I find friends?	**18** I am starving myself to fit into size two jeans. Will it be worth it?	**19** If I drink alcoholic beverages, I'll eat less food and lose weight. Agree or disagree. Why?	**20** I don't measure up to movie or music stars or sports heroes. What can I do?
21 I want a weight lifter body but I'm too lazy. What can I do?	**22** No one likes me because I look different. How can I be accepted?	**23** I want plastic surgery to reshape my nose so I will have more friends. What will my new friends be like?	**24** Should I change my appearance to please others? Why or why not?	**25** I feel unlucky. People with good looks and money get all the breaks. How will I get some good luck?

TEENS – Body Image and Beyond

Dear Advice Columnist …

FOR THE FACILITATOR

I. Purpose
To consider situations related to looks, dating, popularity and obtain peer feedback.

II. General Comments
Teens often sacrifice health, sanity and individuality at any cost to seek social acceptance.

III. Possible Activities

1. Individual Activity

Distribute the *Dear Advice Columnist . . .* handout and ask teens to write their advice on a separate paper and/or share their ideas orally.

2. Game Using Cut -Outs
  a. Before session, photocopy handout, cut apart *Advice Columnist* squares; fold, and place them in a container.
  b. Ask teens about their experiences writing to or reading responses from advice columnists.
  c. Teens take turns sitting at the front of the room and reading a cut-out from the container.
  d. Peers offer brief opinions and advice without questioning the person.

3. Game Using Teen Created Letters
  a. Distribute blank slips of paper; teens write short anonymous letters asking advice about situations they face related to looks and body image, (involving dating, sports, etc.).
  b. Allow time for completion, then collect folded slips and place them into a container.
  c. Teens take turns reading and giving advice (as in the game using cut-outs above).

NUMBERS 1 & 2 ABOVE, advice corresponding to numbers on cut-outs may include these ideas:

1. You are not inferior because of body build; you may need a partner who appreciates who you are.
2. Find females who like brains not brawn, who may be similarly interested in intellectual pursuits.
3. Be assertive; talk with a trusted adult.
4. Dangerous side effects; brief weight loss; find people who like you, not a number on your scale.
5. Talk with the friend, say No to the borrowing; help with fashion suggestions; shop together.
6. Determine if complaints are valid; discuss with your family your more important traits.
7. Some romances start as friendships; stop acting like *one of the guys*; seek different types of males.
8. Encourage friends to have empathy and be open to diversity; if it continues, consider new friends.
9. Dangerous side-effects; often illegal; short-lived results; instead, exercise, practice, eat right.
10. Find a girlfriend in an art class, gallery, or art organization; all females don't look for athletes.
11. Look your best, be yourself, stop comparisons; seek friends with similar interests and values.
12. If your partner leaves because of someone's looks, let your partner go.
13. Consider the validity of their concerns, (dirty? gang attire?); discuss your friends' good points.
14. Dangerous; illegal; weight gain when you stop using speed; get proper nutrition and exercise.
15. Focus on your unique strengths and personality and find like-minded friends.
16. Acceptance with true friends is not based on fashion; attractive dress need not be expensive.
17. People may be jealous or may sense conceit; get your mind off yourself; be interested in others.
18. Starving ruins physical and mental health and when you resume eating, the jeans no longer fit.
19. You might eat more due to decreased inhibitions; it's dangerous and liver disease swells bellies.
20. Stop unrealistic comparisons; be the best you that you can be; work on enduring traits and goals.
21. Get up and work out, or decide on different goals; develop your mind instead of muscles, etc.
22. Celebrate your individuality; become a champion for people with distinctions.
23. Plastic surgery won't fix your life or personality; you will gain only temporary friends.
24. You will never please everyone; develop personal goals, unique style and internal attributes.
25. They may be favored; you can make your own luck through positive thinking and hard work.

IV. Enrichment Activities
Teens share the best advice they ever received, (not necessarily related to body image).

My Profile ▶

BODY BIAS BINGO

B 1-10	I 11-20	N 21-30	G 31-40	O 41-50
How does body bias affect relationships and popularity?	How does the media touch up images?	How have models suffered by the current thinking that *Thin is In*?	Name a celebrity famous mostly for face, figure and fashion.	What can be learned from a beautiful actor who didn't get surgery on her nose?
What magazines promote thinness, muscles and good looks? How?	Which dolls and mannequins promote unrealistic ideals? How?	What happens when people compare themselves to unrealistic ideals?	Name a celebrity whose talent rather than looks makes him or her famous.	What can be learned from a man born with no right hand who became an Olympic pitcher?
Describe the way most music video stars look and dress.	If someone insults your appearance, what does it mean to *consider the source*?	How would you help a friend who says, *I hate the way I look*.	Name a celebrity with real charitable or humanitarian interests.	What can people do to reduce the power of media madness in their lives?
Describe a typical movie star's facial features and body build.	What types of businesses make money on people's pursuit of thinness, muscles and attractiveness?	What can you suggest to the media to promote realistic images and a range of body sizes?	Describe internal traits you admire in a family member.	How can non-celebrity teens be positive and realistic, true role models, and for whom?
What does this mean? *You can't judge a book by it's cover*.	How can a friend help someone who looks different or has body size issues?	What motivates bullies who mock people who look different?	Describe internal traits you admire in a teacher, coach or counselor.	Describe traits you admire in a person who is in the public eye.

TEENS – Body Image and Beyond

BODY BIAS BINGO
FOR THE FACILITATOR

I. Purpose
To notice and diminish the effects of media on body image.
To compare celebrities known for superficial attributes with meaningful role models.

II. General Comments
Unchallenged, media dictates weight, good looks, hair styles, fashion, popularity, what's cool and what's not. Glossy photos are often air-brushed or otherwise altered. Teens need critical thinking skills about who they admire and why; they need exposure to people who are recognized for what they do versus how they look. Awareness of money making agendas in ads for products to lose weight, gain muscle or fix a feature, is essential.

III. Possible Activities
a. Write on the board: *Media Literacy*. Ask what it means.
   Elicit - the ability to analyze, evaluate and create messages.
b. Encourage brainstorming about the messages bombarding teens today.
c. Distribute *Body Bias BINGO*.
d. Instruct teens to randomly number the boxes (according to the ranges next to each letter).
e. Ideally everyone's numbers will be in different order. Examples:
   - Under B a teen will label the boxes 1-10, in any order.
     Under I – 11-20, in any order
     Under N – 21-30, in any order
     Under G – 31-40, in any order
     Under O – 41-50, in any order
   - Alternatively, the facilitator or a volunteer numbers the pages before group, all pages numbered differently.
f. The BINGO Game:
   - Facilitator calls one number per letter; teens with the number raise hands.
   - Teens read their questions aloud and answer; no rights or wrongs.
   - If a teen cannot respond to the question, peers may assist.
   - After responding, teens color or mark an "X" in the corresponding box.
   - If the same teens keep having lucky numbers, let those who have had no turns call the next numbers, (using numbers they have on their pages).
   - Teens win by answering and marking all boxes in a row horizontally, vertically or diagonally.
   - When someone wins, winner calls the numbers as peers continue to play.
   - At session's end, if no one won, the teen with the most marked numbers wins.

IV. Enrichment Activities
Discuss celebrities and their charities.

My Profile ▶

I-Messages

E-mails, texts, instant messages, voice mail, blogs, etc. are quick but permanent.

I–Messages are self-talk that can either build you up or tear you down.

Have you ever been in an awful mood that suddenly turned good for seemingly no reason? Have you ever been in a great mood that suddenly turned bad for seemingly no reason? Probably an *I-Message* or thought about yourself popped into your head. Thoughts about personal feelings and ideas, or *I-Messages*, can be changed before becoming indelibly imprinted on your brain. **Monitor your I-Messages; delete negatives, save positives!** See examples below; then write your terrible and terrific body image thoughts. Notice the effects on your feelings and actions.

EXAMPLE:

I-Message (Thought)	Feelings	Actions
Terrible I-Message I feel like a wimp around jocks.	Inferiority, unhappiness.	Avoid people with better builds.
Terrific I-Message They have muscles, I have skills.	Equality, satisfaction.	Socialize with people I like, not comparing my muscles with theirs.

NOW YOU DO IT:

Terrible I-Message		
Terrific I-Message		

Terrible I-Message		
Terrific I-Message		

Terrible I-Message		
Terrific I-Message		

Terrible I-Message		
Terrific I-Message		

TEENS – Body Image and Beyond

I-Messages

FOR THE FACILITATOR

I. Purpose
To make an analogy between electronic messages and self-talk.

To change negative thoughts to positive but realistic I-Messages and note the changes in emotions and behavior.

II. General Comments
Cognitive therapy is effective in changing distorted ideas about body image and appearance. Teens practice changing I-Messages that they use to tear themselves down to thoughts that can build them up.

III. Possible Activities
a. Write the words I-Message on the board and check for group members' understanding.
b. Distribute the I-Message handout.
c. Teens take turns reading the information and examples aloud; then complete the page.
d. Teens take turns sharing their Terrible I-Messages; peers suggest positive changes.
e. Then the teen who is sharing reads his or her own Terrific I-Messages.
f. 0Teens need not share messages they consider private.

IV. Enrichment Activities
a. Write the statements on the board, one at a time;
   (elicit changes similar to italicized suggestions):
   - I believe I am ugly.   *I have attractive inner traits.*
   - I feel clumsy around cheerleaders.   *I'm adept at art.*
   - My face isn't perfect.   *I find ways to enhance my personality.*
   - My body is not maturing fast enough or too fast.   *Individual growth patterns vary.*
   - The popular people look better than me.   *I look and act my best.*
   - I try to seem mature by dressing like an adult.   *It's better to act more mature and dress my age.*
   - I eat lots but am still too thin.   *I have decided to emphasize my slim build.*
   - No matter how much I diet, I cannot be thin.   *I am content with my curves.*
   - I dislike my pale skin and constantly go to tanning booth or the beach.   *I'll accept my skin tone rather than have skin cancer or early wrinkles.*
b. Encourage a discussion regarding physical changes that can be made. Emphasize this would be to raise self-confidence rather than to fit into a mold of perfection perpetuated by media standards. Elicit examples from teens or select from the list; avoid those that might embarrass participants:
   - Acne – Medication and skin treatments.
   - Misshapen nose or other feature – Plastic surgery.
   - Over or under weight – Nutritional plan and exercise, in moderation.
   - Body shape issues – clothes to highlight assets and downplay flaws.
   - Minor skin conditions – Make-up and over the counter products.
c. Discuss how teens might access some of the above interventions:
   - Insurance, depending on plan coverage.
   - Low cost clinics for medical or dental care.
   - Teens working part-time to cover some of the costs.
d. Encourage discussion or debates regarding:
   - If you fix a feature will it fix your life? Why or why not?
   - What might be going on inside someone who had too many cosmetic surgeries?

My Profile

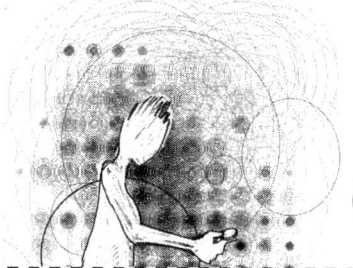

Coin a Phrase

1 Public opinion is a weak tyrant compared with our own private opinion. ~ Henry David Thoreau	**2** Treat yourself as if you already are what you'd like to be. ~Wayne Dyer	**3** I believe that your head is the only thing in your way. ~ Christina Perri song lyrics	**4** True popularity comes from acts of kindness rather than acts of stupidity. ~ Bo Bennett
5 Every storm runs, runs out of rain, Just like every dark night turns into day. ~ Gary Allan song lyrics	**6** Be thine own palace or the world's thy jail. ~ John Donne	**7** We know who we are, but not what we may be. ~ William Shakespeare	**8** Wanting to be someone else is a waste of who you are. ~ Marilyn Monroe
9 The worst loneliness is to not be comfortable with yourself. ~ Mark Twain	**10** Find out what makes your heart sing and create your own music. ~ Mac Anderson	**11** First say to yourself what you would be; then do what you have to do. ~ Epictetus	**12** I would rather be damned by my honesty, than caged by my lies. ~ Omega Maverick
13 Integrity simply means not violating one's own identity. ~Eric Fromm	**14** Men can starve from a lack of self-realization as much as… from a lack of bread. ~ Richard Wright	**15** The best way to find yourself is in the service of others. ~ Mahatma Gandhi	**16** Don't you see the starlight, starlight? Don't you dream impossible things? ~ Taylor Swift song lyrics
17 The road to self belief is potholed. ~ Nyasha Madavo	**18** Look inside yourself Like your oldest friend Just trust the voice within. ~ Christina Aguilera song lyrics	**19** Knowing who you are is the best defense against who they think you are. ~ Dodinsky	**20** When your heart speaks, take good notes. ~ Judith Campbell
21 I spend a lot of time trying not to be me. So much so that I have become who I am not. ~Jarod Kintz	**22** An identity would seem to be arrived at by the way in which a person faces and uses his experience. ~ James Baldwin	**23** Man cannot remake himself without suffering, for he is both the marble and the sculptor. ~ Dr. Alexis Carrel	**24** There was a time when the risk to remain tight in the bud was more painful than the risk it took to blossom. ~Anais Nin

TEENS – Body Image and Beyond

Coin a Phrase

FOR THE FACILITATOR

I. **Purpose**

   To consider identity aspects aside from looks, popularity, achievements or a public persona. To use kindness, service, experience, risks, self-knowledge, aspirations, etc., to define unique selfhood.

II. **General Comments**

   By playing a game with quotations, teens incorporate character into their *profiles*.

III. **Possible Activities**

   a. Before session, photocopy and cut out the quotes and scatter them on the floor, blank side up, in the center or front of room. If time permits, tape each onto an index card.
   b. Allow as much space between them as possible.
   c. Teens take turns standing a few feet away, tossing a coin or game chip onto the floor, trying to land on a cut-out.
   d. Teens pick up the cut-out quote closest to where their coin or game chip landed and read it aloud.
   e. The teens apply the quotes to their own identity and receive peer feedback; or peers may relate the quote themselves.
   f. The game continues until all cut-out quotes have been used.

IV. **Enrichment activities**

   Ask these questions after teens apply the quotes to their identities. (Numbers on cut-outs correspond to questions below).

   1. Why is your own opinion of yourself more important and harsher than opinions of others?
   2. How can you treat yourself differently?
   3. How might you change your thinking to clear your path?
   4. Give an example of foolish acts you have done to win approval.
   5. As your storm runs out of rain, what does your day look like?
   6. How will you become your own *palace, fortress or stronghold*?
   7. Think – *the sky is the limit*; who might you be or become?
   8. In what ways have you wasted who you are?
   9. How are you becoming comfortable with yourself?
   10. What makes your heart sing?
   11. To be what you want to be, what do you have to do?
   12. How could lies cage you?
   13. Share one way you will not violate your identity.
   14. How are you working toward reaching your potential?
   15. How might you be of service to others?
   16. What dream is in your starlight and no longer light years away?
   17. Describe a current pothole on your road to self-belief.
   18. What positive action is your voice within urging you to do?
   19. What do you know about yourself that helps you ignore unjust opinions of you?
   20. What is your heart telling you?
   21. In what ways have you almost become who you are not?
   22. Share how you faced and used a recent experience.
   23. What is uncomfortable about remolding yourself?
   24. Name one risk that is helping you blossom.

MY FRIENDS 2

> Friends...
> They cherish one another's hopes.
> They are kind to one another's dreams.
> — HENRY DAVID THOREAU

BIGGER THAN .... page 25 ▶
By seeing how others turned adversity into altruism, teens identify priorities beyond popularity, looks, and romance.

MY SOLAR SYSTEM .... page 27 ▶
Teens depict significant people in their universe, their emotional proximity or distance; they decide what their lives revolve around and whether to change their sun.

STAYING POWER .... page 29 ▶
Teens identify internal qualities that surpass superficial appeal.

Friends Don't Squelch or Squash .... page 31 ▶
Teens recognize insincere friends who try to silence or inhibit their growth.

My Friends

BIGGER THAN . . .
People's potential for greatness often emerges from adversity.

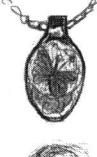
1. An artist creates three dimensional designs on spoon pendants. Her jewelry company has its roots in her eating disorder; making collages was part of her therapy.

2. A man lost his son, an aspiring pro golfer, to drug addiction. He organized a memorial tournament that raises money for an addiction recovery program.

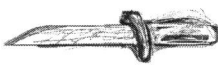
3. A young woman broke up with her boyfriend who later raped her at knifepoint and shot her in the face. She teaches teens about dating violence prevention and pushed for legislation in Ohio to allow juvenile courts to issue protective orders to minors in abusive dating relationships.

4. A basketball star, suffered due to his mother's addiction. His dad raised him and he now reveres his own parental role. He wrote a great book about he himself being a father and how important it is to him. His mom is now a drug free pastor, helping children.

After reading the information above, what is the common theme? _____
_____
_____

How might you use a difficulty to help others? _____
_____
_____

Something might seem overly important to you (looks, grades, popularity, sports, a romance, etc.). Fill in the blank: *I am bigger than* _____
_____
_____

What piece of you would you like to take priority in your life? Fill in the blank: *I am a* _____
_____
_____ first.

TEENS – Body Image and Beyond

BIGGER THAN . . .
FOR THE FACILITATOR

I. Purpose
To recognize that altruism often stems from adversity.

To decide whether body image, popularity, romance or another issue is dominating a teen's life and replace it with a more enduring value or role.

II. General Comments
Teen friends need not be limited to school, work, neighborhood or social networking sites. They may seek out other *friends* (role models) people who make the world a better place versus obsessing about a better body, face, or other superficial achievement.

III. Possible Activities
a. Write *Friends* on the board and ask teens how they develop new friends.
b. Suggest they can find people they admire by reading biographies, searching websites, etc.
c. Distribute *Bigger Than . . .* handout.
d. Ask teens to brainstorm commonalities among the four people listed.
Response to elicit: These people cared about others and used adversity to their advantage. They made lemonade out of lemons.
e. Allow time for teens to individually complete the page.
f. Encourage teens to share their responses and receive peer feedback.

IV. Enrichment Activities
a. Encourage teens to brainstorm issues that could destroy them or make them stronger.
b. A volunteer lists their ideas on the board.
Examples to elicit include the already addressed problems (eating disorders, death of a loved one, violent attacks, and parental addiction) plus possibilities such as the following:
- Body image disturbances, disfigurement and disabilities.
- Being a victim of childhood abuse, or dysfunctional family issues.
- Being bullied or shunned by peers.
- Unrelenting external pressure to be something against one's better judgment.
- Broken romances or friendships.
- Poor grades or losing a game, contest or competition.

c. Discuss altruistic activities teens might do alone or with friends who have common goals. Examples to elicit include the following:
- Food, clothing, book, can or bottle drives; items or funds go to needy people or charitable organizations.
- Visit or send cards to burn victims or people in hospitals or rehab facilities.
- Volunteer at animal shelters, homeless shelters and food programs.
- Organize panels to teach people about the issue; make posters and flyers, etc.

My Friends

MY SOLAR SYSTEM

For this exercise, you are the sun, at the center of your solar system. The people in your life are planets.

In the square below depict with circles:

1. Around you are significant people in your life.
2. Portray their positions or emotional proximity to you.
3. Draw each person's circle, close, in the middle, or at the edge of the paper, etc., according to their relational bonds with you (use code names)
4. Label the circles using name-codes.

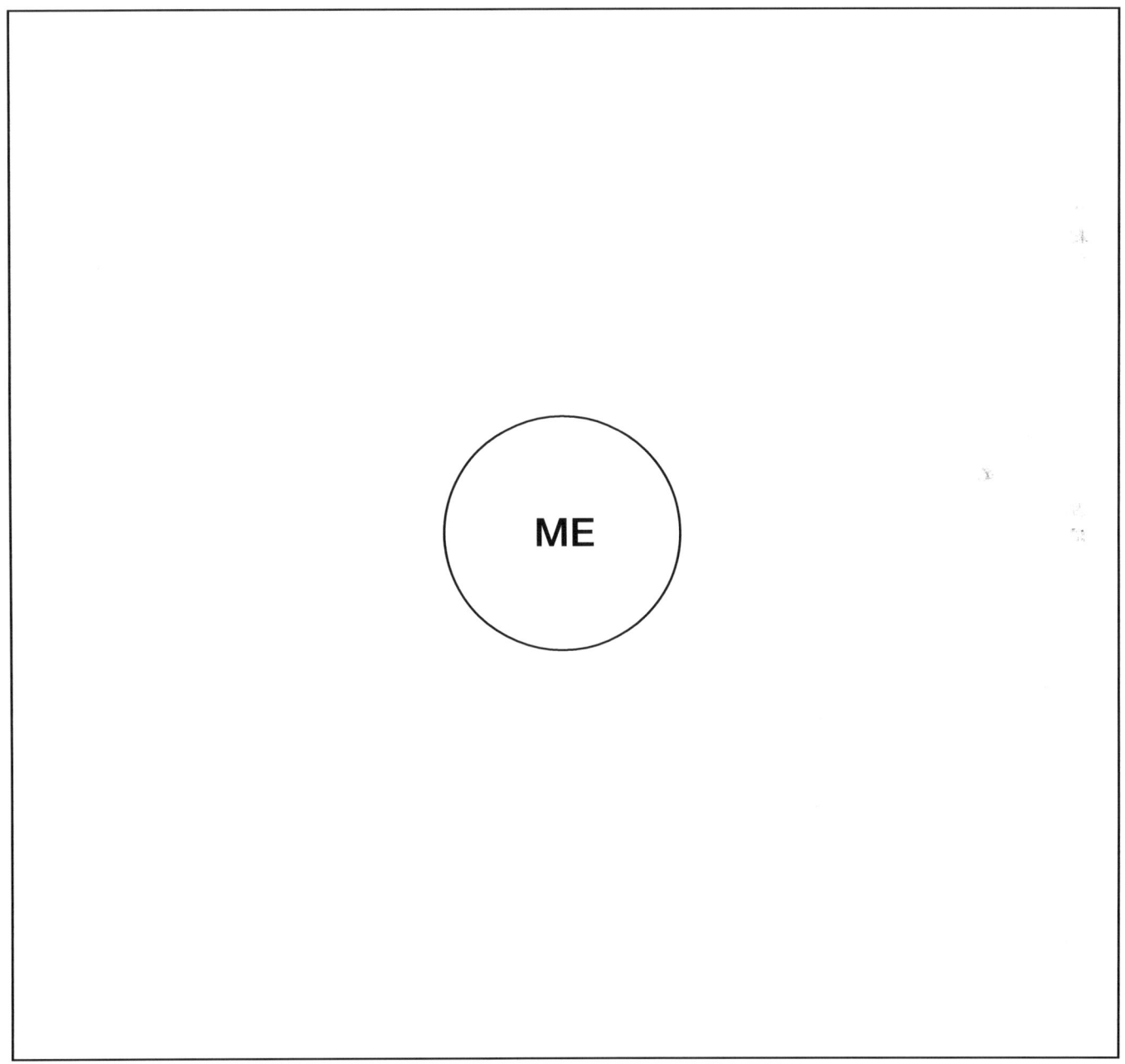

MY SOLAR SYSTEM

FOR THE FACILITATOR

I. **Purpose**

   To identify friends, family and significant others in terms of emotional closeness.

   To determine whether superficial bonds or deeper connections exist.

II. **General Comments**

   Teens may feel isolated or smothered or somewhere in between. They may be valued for appearance or performance or loved unconditionally. They will identify who needs to be more distant or closer.

III. **Possible Activities**
   a. Write *Solar System* on the board and elicit that planets orbit around the sun in various distances.
   b. Tell them they will pretend they are the center of their universe during this activity.
   c. Ask what it means for someone to be *in your space* or *crowding* it.
   d. Encourage a discussion of the opposite: people so emotionally removed they don't hear your cries or voice. Elicit that geography has no relevance; they might live in the same house with someone who is an emotional stranger, or frequently communicate with a soul mate across the country.
   e. Distribute the *My Solar System* handout and allow time for completion. (Remind teens to use code names).
   f. Encourage teens to share their drawings; identify which bonds are superficial (based on appearance, money, etc.) and which are deep (based on mutual respect, authenticity, etc.)
   g. Ask teens to identify persons they wish were closer to, or further away from them.

IV. **Enrichment Activities**
   a. Ask teens to identify something misleading in the *My Solar System* activity.
      Elicit that they are not the center of the universe and people do not revolve around them.
   b. Encourage them to brainstorm people and/or things and situations that their lives might revolve around.
      Possible examples are listed below.
      People:
      - A dating partner
      - A team
      - A friend, clique, or gang
      - A celebrity
      - A person they idolize

      Things and Situations:
      - Their body or face
      - Their weight or musculature
      - Their food
      - Alcohol or drugs
      - Money, clothes, cars, material items
      - Winning in sports; performance in cheerleading, scholastics; other talents
   c. Ask teens what happens if any person or thing becomes their *sun*.
      Elicit that people, popularity, looks, money, etc., are transient. Being at the top of one's game or the head of the class doesn't last forever.
   d. Encourage teens to identify values that their lives might revolve around such as empathy, creativity, generosity, working for social or political causes, faith, etc.

My Friends

STAYING POWER

Check your traits that make you a good friend and give you staying power with others.

- ❏ **Be the real deal** – I embrace my uniqueness and imperfections.
- ❏ **Encourage and empathize** – I make people feel better with my words.
- ❏ **Stick up for friends, underdogs, partners, etc.** – I do not backstab or cheat.
- ❏ **Thank others** – I appreciate when people help me or do good deeds.
- ❏ **Be thankful** – I focus on my positive attributes, not my flaws.
- ❏ **Laugh out loud** – I laugh, even at myself, when necessary.
- ❏ **Give** – I give my time, expertise, money or energy to a cause or by helping others.
- ❏ **Blaze** – I am on fire doing my best.

Add any additional qualities you possess:

- _____
- _____
- _____

Add any additional qualities you would like to possess:

- _____
- _____
- _____

A friend in need is a friend in deed.

Write about a time when you were in need of a friend who helped you.

_____
_____
_____

Write about a time when you helped a friend in need.

_____
_____
_____

TEENS – Body Image and Beyond

STAYING POWER
FOR THE FACILITATOR

I. **Purpose**
   To develop and reinforce teen qualities that surpasses superficial appeal.

II. **General Comments**
   Teens are better served by friendships based on honesty, empathy, loyalty, appreciation and generosity. Laughing, especially at oneself, and pursuing a passion are attractive attributes.

III. **Possible Activities**
   a. Write *Fair-weather Friends* on the board and encourage a discussion of its meaning, (people who support you when it is pleasant, profitable, convenient; they become escape artists when times are tough or you are in trouble).
   b. Ask teens to brainstorm qualities of true friends.
   c. A volunteer lists teens' ideas on the board.
   d. Distribute the *Staying Power* handout and allow time for completion.
   e. Encourage teens to tell about their traits and their *Friend in Need* responses.

IV. **Enrichment Activities**
   a. Encourage teens to identify which trait on the checklist they best exemplify and how.
   - Ask teens to share any additional traits they listed.
   b. Write on the board the Friedrich Nietzsche quote:

   Love is blind; friendship closes its eyes.

   - Ask teens to analyze the quote and share times they closed their eyes to a friend's faults or a friend overlooked their shortcomings.
   - Remind teens to use code names and/or disguise friends' identities.

My Friends

Friends Don't Squelch or Squash

Consider this quote and complete the thoughts below (use name codes).

> No person is your friend who demands your silence or denies your right to grow.
> ~ Alice Walker

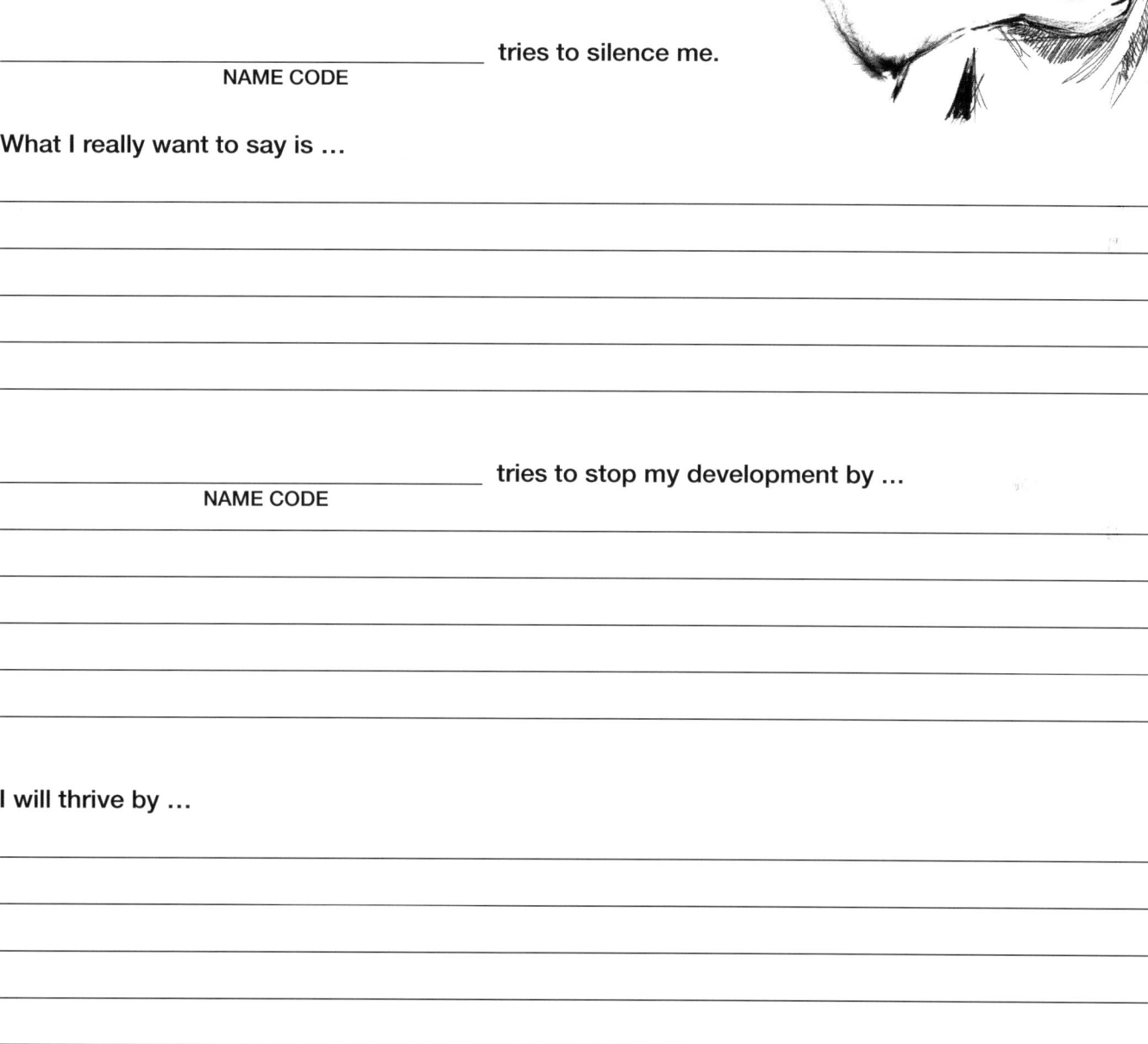

_____ tries to silence me.
NAME CODE

What I really want to say is …

_____
_____
_____
_____
_____

_____ tries to stop my development by …
NAME CODE

_____
_____
_____
_____
_____

I will thrive by …

_____
_____
_____
_____

TEENS – Body Image and Beyond

Friends Don't Squelch or Squash

FOR THE FACILITATOR

I. Purpose

To recognize insincere friends who hush teens' voices or inhibit them.

To freely express important thoughts and flourish despite opposition.

II. General Comments

Teens need freedom to speak, do, and be the best person they are capable of becoming. They will recognize that people who are not true friends will diminish their beliefs, opinions and aspirations. Teens need to rise above inhibiting influences.

III. Possible Activities

a. Walk into the room with masking tape on your mouth and your hands tied. (Do not ask a teen to do this as it might be considered abusive).

b. Untie your hands, take off the tape, and ask teens what you were portraying. Response to elicit: Being speechless and helpless and then finding a way to feel free.

c. Encourage a discussion about ways people squelch or squash them. Possibilities:

- Peer pressure to avoid talking to certain people or to not express controversial opinions.
- Peer pressure to reject other people because they are different.
- Fear of being outcast because their opinion differs from leaders or other members of a clique.
- People dissuading them from joining clubs or extracurricular activities not considered cool by their clique.
- People mocking their efforts in scholastics, sports, the arts or other endeavors.
- Possibly parents who disallow divergent views or frown upon the teens' aspirations.
- People who thwart teens' ambitions because of jealousy or other motives.

d. Distribute the *Friends Don't Squelch or Squash* handout and allow time for completion.

e. Encourage teens to share their responses.

IV. Enrichment Activities

a. Encourage teens to share instances when they tried to suppress a friend's thoughts or belittle a friend's goals.

b. Ask them to brainstorm times when silence actually is or was golden. Possibilities:

- When speaking would break a confidence (except if suicide, homicide, or abuse has been revealed).
- When speaking would involve damaging gossip.
- When speaking in anger would be regretted later.
- When an upset friend needs to express feelings to someone who will listen.
- When your silence alone is enough.

MY GENES AND MY JEANS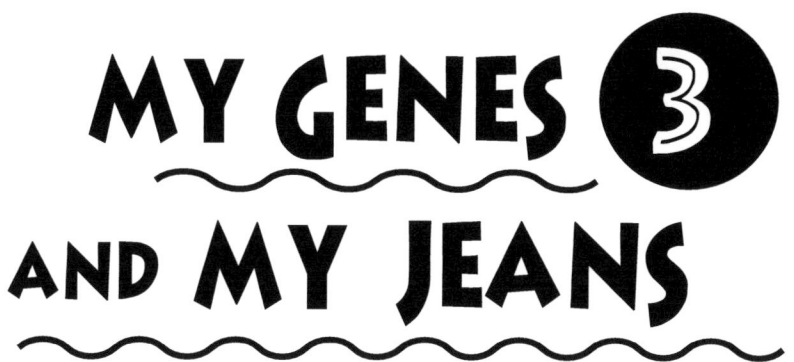

Life consists not simply in what heredity and environment do to us but in what we make out of what they do to us.

— Harry Emerson Fosdick

Morphs that Don't .... page 35 ▶
Teens explore the role of heredity and acceptance regarding body types; they decide what can be changed through healthy lifestyles.

Trait-agories .... page 37 ▶
Instead of focusing on face and physique, teens share how they exemplify leadership, friendship, positive personality traits and success.

My Genes and My Jeans

Morphs that Don't

You have inherited a certain body-type, or possibly a combination of body-types.

See the descriptions below and draw the body types.

Go with the flow if you are artistic, or draw… a stick figure and pad it; a gingerbread cookie shaped as described; a cartoon or caricature.

Ectomorph	**Endomorph**	**Mesomorph**
Long and lean; flat chest; thin bones; narrow hips and shoulders.	Curvy; weight in hips and thighs on females; love handles on males; short limbs, small hands and feet	Muscular; strong bones; females have hourglass shapes; males have rectangular builds
No matter how much I eat, I just can't gain weight!	*I look at food and seem to gain weight!*	*I build bulk without much effort.*

Which body type most closely describes you? _____

What are the advantages of your body type? _____

What aspects of your shape might you have to learn to like? _____

What happens when people try to change the body type they were born to be? _____

TEENS – Body Image and Beyond

Morphs that Don't

FOR THE FACILITATOR

I. Purpose
To identify the role of heredity in determining basic body build.
To consider advantages and acceptance of one's own physique.

II. General Comments
Our DNA makes us who we are to an extent, but this can be improved. Trying to make drastic changes can make people miserable as they fight an uphill battle all of their life.

III. Possible Activities
a. Ask teens to share who they resemble in their family; if adopted and have no knowledge of their biological parents, what clues do they have by looking at themselves?

b. Encourage brainstorming of typical inherited traits.

Response to elicit: similar nose, legs, teeth, weight, height, hair color, eye color, etc.

c. Distribute the *Morphs that Don't* handout and allow time for completion.

d. Encourage teens to share their drawings and responses.

IV. Enrichment Activities
a. Make three columns on the board; headings are *Ecto, Endo* and *Meso*.
   - Either as a group, or in three teams, (one body-type per team), teens list celebrities or people in history who exemplify each shape.

b. Encourage discussion of Nature versus Nurture

Nature influences:

- How people capture, store and release energy from food; genes may impact hunger and energy levels for exercise.
- In many experiments (and in real life) overweight people lose weight but regain it; their bodies sense starvation and conserve calories.
- Many thin people, who gained weight for an experiment, often lost it effortlessly.
- It is theorized that metabolism speeds up or slows down to maintain the weight considered normal for each person's inborn build.
- People may have a range within ten to twenty pounds to manipulate; gaining or losing beyond those limits may be resisted by the body.
- Adoptees, in adulthood, resembled biological parents' body types.
- Twins often had nearly identical weights in adulthood, whether reared apart or together.

Nurture influences:

- Emotional eating (as a reward, or when sad, overwhelmed, stressed, etc.) and food preferences; culture affects attitudes and choices.
- Sedentary or active lifestyles may be modeled and promoted.
- Selecting certain foods (if available in the environment) adequate sleep, and stepped up exercise will decrease a tendency to gain weight.

c. Help teens recognize that **genes cannot be changed but healthy choices maximize their potential to be in the best shape possible for their genetic make-up.**

My Genes and My Jeans

Trait-agories

Leadership

1. Share a time you showed **judgment** by thinking about a situation versus making a snap decision.
2. Share a time you were **dependable** by doing your best on a task you disliked or disagreed with.
3. Share a time you showed **initiative** by doing something without being asked to do it.
4. Share a time you gained **knowledge** by asking, listening, watching, reading or trying something.
5. Share a time you showed **loyalty** by sticking up for a person or a belief.

Friendship and Compassion

1. Share a time you demonstrated **empathy** by putting yourself in another person's shoes.
2. Share a time you were **positive** by thinking the best of people, giving the benefit of the doubt.
3. Share a time you were **respectful** by disagreeing with someone without degrading the person.
4. Share ways you are **approachable** regarding your facial expression and body language.
5. Share ways you are **involved**, or will be, in activities where you will meet like-minded people.

Personality

1. Share your tendency toward **extroversion** (people-oriented) or **introversion** (prefer solitude).
2. Share a time you were **agreeable**; share a time you were **disagreeable**. Which are you usually?
3. Share an example of your **conscientiousness**, being goal-directed & organized, following through.
4. Share a time you were **adventurous** by trying a new experience outside your comfort zone.
5. Share a time you were **creative** by either using your imagination or finding a unique solution.

Success

1. Share a time you showed **humility** by admitting you were wrong.
2. Share a time you were **courageous** by taking a risk, failing temporarily, but gaining wisdom.
3. Share a time you were **persistent** by not giving up when the going got tough.
4. Share a time you were **tactful** by thinking before speaking or not criticizing.
5. Share a time you were **generous** by giving credit due to others or sharing the limelight.

TEENS – Body Image and Beyond

Trait-agories

FOR THE FACILITATOR

I. **Purpose**

To look beyond the build of a body to intangible traits; to recognize some positive aspects of personality.

To identify qualities needed for leadership, friendship, and success.

II. **General Comments**

Teens often focus on physical traits; they need ways to define themselves in terms of interpersonal and intra-personal attributes. *Trait-agories* is a question and answer game with trait-related categories.

III. **Possible Activities**

   a. Photocopy and cut the reproducible page on the broken lines.
   b. Discuss that like physical characteristics, personality and behavioral traits are partly genetic and partly acquired. (Twins reared apart score similarly on tests; yet people do develop skills).
   c. List the categories on the board – *Leadership, Friendship, Personality,* and *Success.*
   d. Ask for four volunteers who are comfortable reading aloud.
   e. Explain they will be reading the trait prompts to players (peers) when their topic is picked.
   f. Ask volunteers to choose a topic; distribute prompts for the topic chosen.
   g. The four questioners sit at the front of the room.
   h. Explain that the players will take turns selecting a topic and responding to a trait prompt.
   i. Players select a topic and the questioner with that topic reads one of the prompts.
   j. Emphasize that there are no right or wrong answers; teens say what is true for them.
   k. Once all five prompts in a category have been responded to, cross the word off the board; ask players to select from the remaining topics.
   l. If all twenty prompts are responded to and time remains, they may start all over; advise players to select a different topic the second time around.

IV. **Enrichment Activities**

   a. Encourage a discussion of other traits teens consider important; possibilities include enthusiasm, unselfishness, a sense of fairness, forgiveness, etc.
   b. Write *Interests and Abilities* on the board and ask teens to brainstorm types; list their ideas.

   Possibilities:
   - Interest in plants, geology, weather, health etc.; being a nature-lover.
   - Ability to sing, play an instrument, compose music or lyrics; appreciating music.
   - Being a math *wizard*; loving numbers and number games.
   - People skills, empathy, active listening; enjoying social events.
   - Athletic prowess, coordination, balance, physical strength; loving dance, sports or exercise.
   - Writing prose, poetry, articles for school papers, etc.; reading avidly.
   - Spiritual strengths, ability to self-soothe; faith in people and circumstances.
   - Artistic ability; proficient in crafts, decorating; appreciating paintings, sculptures, etc.
   - Dramatic ability; comedy, writing and directing; enjoying theater arts.
   - Interest in animals; ability to train animals; caring for pets, learning about zoology.
   - Being a good friend, caring, listening, trustworthy.

   c. Encourage teens to identify their strengths in the above (and additional) categories.

SHAPE, SIZE AND SPORTS 4

> I've missed more than 9,000 shots in my career.
> I've lost almost 300 games.
> 26 times I've been trusted to take the winning shot and missed.
> I've failed over and over and over again in my life.
> And that is why I succeed.
>
> — MICHAEL JORDAN

SHAPES AND SPORTS .... page 41 ▶
Teens connect the banana, apple, pear and yam to specific sports; ponder priorities: perfection, performance or physical and mental health; and identify ways to handle sports set-backs.

Steer Away: Steroids and Male Athletes .... page 43 ▶
Males depict physical, mental, and image-impairing effects from steroids and growth hormones.

Pain and NO Gain: Steroids and Female Athletes .... page 45 ▶
Females depict the dangers of steroids.

Mirrors and Muscles .... page 47 ▶
From illustrations, teens identify behaviors associated with Muscle Dysmorphia; features of the Female Athlete Triad are discussed.

What is Sportsmanship? .... page 49 ▶
By playing a letter and word game, teens personalize sportsmanship slogans and apply motivational quotations to their lives.

Shapes and Sports

Can a short person make the basketball team? Can a featherweight play football?

Can a gymnast or swimmer be plump? Athletes can defy the rules, but body types are usually suited to specific sports.

Examples:

- **The Banana** is slim, neither curvy nor muscle bound, suited for endurance sports like running, swimming, soccer; if tall – basketball; if short – gymnastics.

- **The Apple** is round through the middle, muscular, suited for strength-related sports like wrestling, and football.

- **The Pear's** weight is mostly in the lower half of the body and is suited for martial arts, and short distance endurance like baseball and volleyball.

- **The Yam** is big and strong and is suited for power sports like football.

In what sports do you do well or might you excel in the future?

_____
_____
_____

If sports are unimportant to you, how does your body type help you in activities that matter to you?

_____
_____
_____

If you don't make it onto a team or are eliminated due to weight or performance, describe three positive ways to look at it and act.

_____
_____

TEENS – Body Image and Beyond

SHAPES AND SPORTS

FOR THE FACILITATOR

I. Purpose
   To link body types to sports or other meaningful activities and discuss pressures from coaches, parents and peers.
   To plan positive ways to cope with not being selected or being eliminated from a team.

II. General Comments
   Although sports promote fitness, teamwork, good sportsmanship and academic standards to stay on the team, some coaches, parents and peers pressure teens to gain or lose weight and win at any cost to their well-being.

III. Possible Activities
   1. If possible have an actual banana, apple, pear and yam available; alternately ask volunteers to draw them on the board.

   2. Reveal that the session's topic is sports and ask teens why they are seeing or drawing fruit and a vegetable.

   3. Distribute the *Shapes and Sports* handout and allow time for completion.

   4. Ask volunteers to share their work and insights.

   5. Encourage brainstorming about life lessons learned from sports.

IV. Enrichment Activities
   a. Encourage a discussion about famous athletes who gained and lost medals and popularity due to illegal or unethical behavior; examples include athletes who use drugs, purposefully injure opponents, are involved in infidelity; participate in illegal gambling, etc.

   b. Being a star athlete or cheerleader promotes popularity. Ask whether too much importance is placed on these. Encourage a discussion regarding other teen accomplishments that need to be recognized in schools and society and ways to promote them.

   c. Share the following with teens: Gymnastics, ice skating, ballet, and some other activities push thinness. Encourage a discussion with the teens of their own experiences with parents, coaches or peers who prioritize perfection, weight, and performance over mental and physical well-being. Remind group members to use name codes.

   d. Encourage a discussion about famous athletes who improve the world, like the runner stricken with cancer who ran marathons to raise research money, or the football player who turned down a multi-million dollar contract to fight the War on Terror.

   e. Ask teens to brainstorm sports stars whose body shapes resemble the banana, apple, pear and yam.

Shape, Size and Sports

Steer Away: Steroids and Male Athletes

Males may be tempted to illegally take anabolic steroids and growth hormones, to bulk up their bodies, make them look more masculine and be better in sports; however, opposite and worse effects may occur.

On the right draw possible steroid effects. Be creative!

- Bloating
- Depression
- Early baldness
- Irritability, angry face
- Jaundice (yellow skin)
- Liver and kidney tumors
- Low sperm count
- Skin issues
- Stunted growth
- Trembling hands

Add Growth Hormone effects:

- Enlarged heart
- Overgrown bones, hands and feet
- Protruding brows and jaw

Be aware that emotional and social effects include: mood swings, manic agitation, depression, paranoia, jealousy, feeling invincible, poor judgment, learning and memory problems, plus the humiliation of being suspended or eliminated from teams, giving up awards, and potential legal consequences.

TEENS – Body Image and Beyond

Steer Away: Steroids and Male Athletes
FOR THE FACILITATOR

I. Purpose
To learn the image-impairing effects of steroids and growth hormones by depicting them.

To discuss emotional and medical problems from steroids and growth hormones.

II. General Comments
Young males feel pressure to be big, strong and sexy; they think anabolic steroids and growth hormones enhance athletic ability and masculinity. Effects on body image, emotions, social consequences and medical conditions are addressed.

III. Possible Activities
a. The session will ideally include males only due to discussion of sexual effects; if males and females are in session, use different hand-outs for each gender.

b. At the facilitator's discretion, write these effects on the reproducible page before photocopying:
- Breast and nipple growth
- Shrinking testicles
- Impotence, inability to get an erection

c. Write on the board *roids* and *juice* and ask participants what they mean, (street names for steroids); ask participants about their experiences – being tempted or trying steroids or growth hormones.

d. Distribute the *Steer Away: Steroids and Male* Athletes handout and allow time for completion.

e. If both genders are together, distribute the *Steer Away: Steroids and Male Athletes* to young men; distribute the coordinating handout *Pain and NO Gain: Steroids and Female Athletes* to young women.

f. Encourage a discussion about sports stars and Olympians who were penalized for using these substances.

IV. Enrichment Activities
a. If only males are present, instead of drawing on the reproducible page, have a volunteer draw a big body outline on the board; then teens take turns drawing the effects on the board.

b. Encourage a discussion about other effects: mood swings, manic agitation, depression, paranoia, jealousy, feeling invincible, impaired judgment, learning and memory; greater risk for tendon and ligament injuries, altered blood sugar, impaired thyroid function, heart attacks, blood clots, lowered immunity and other problems.

c. Encourage a discussion regarding whether the body image impairments, emotional or medical effects are worse and why.

d. Teens role play a scenario wherein a coach tells a male he must gain weight and strength for a boxing match quickly. A peer offers him steroids or growth hormones. The boxer portrays what he would do and explains why.

e. Peers provide feedback.

Shape, Size and Sports

Pain and NO Gain: Steroids and Female Athletes

Females may be tempted to take anabolic steroids or growth hormones (illegally) in hopes of building muscle and strength, and enhancing performance. Steroids are more harmful than helpful for females.

On the right draw possible steroid effects on the body. Be creative!

- Blood clots
- Brittle bones
- Development of masculine traits
- Enlarged heart
- Facial and body hair
- Infertility
- Irritability, angry face
- Jaundice (yellow skin)
- Liver and kidney tumors
- Menstrual problems
- Poor wound healing
- Probable eating disorders
- Skin issues
- Stunted growth
- Thin scalp hair
- Uterine cancer

Be aware that emotional and social effects include: mood swings, manic agitation, depression, paranoia, jealousy, feeling invincible, poor judgment, learning and memory problems, plus the humiliation of being suspended or eliminated from teams, giving up awards and potential legal consequences.

TEENS – Body Image and Beyond

Pain and NO Gain: Steroids and Female Athletes

FOR THE FACILITATOR

I. Purpose
To learn the image-impairing effects of steroids by depicting them.
To discuss emotional and medical problems from steroids.

II. General Comments
Steroids are more dangerous to females because their bodies are not equipped to handle male hormones. Also, increased muscle size and strength are not proportional to the amount of male hormones taken; little benefit is seen.

III. Possible Activities
a. The session will ideally include females only due to discussion of sexual effects; if males and females are in session, use different handouts for each gender.
b. At the facilitator's discretion, write these effects on the reproducible page before photocopying:
   - Shrinking breasts
   - Enlarged clitoris
c. Ask teens to describe masculine traits (body and facial hair, deep voice).
d. Ask teens what might cause these in females.
e. Distribute the *Pain and NO Gain: Steroids and Female Athletes* handout and allow time for completion.
f. If both genders are together, distribute the *Pain and NO Gain: Steroids and Female Athletes* handout to young women; distribute the coordinating *Steer Away: Steroids and Male Athletes* handout to young men.
g. Encourage a discussion about sports stars and Olympians who were penalized for using steroids.

IV. Enrichment Activities
a. If only females are present, instead of using the reproducible page, have a volunteer draw a big body outline on the board; then teens take turns drawing effects on the board.
b. Encourage a discussion of other effects: mental instability similar to mania and depression; strokes, heart attacks, lowered immunity; withdrawal effects such as low energy, forgetfulness, confusion, anxiety, and other problems.
c. Encourage a discussion about body image impairments, emotional and medical effects which are worse and why.
d. Teens role play a scenario wherein a coach tells a female she must gain weight and increase muscle and strength to make the team. A peer offers her steroids. The athlete portrays what she would do and explains why.

Shape, Size and Sports

Mirrors and Muscles

**Describe what is happening in each picture.
Muscle Dysmorphia may affect males and females.
Circle any of the pictures in which you see yourself.**

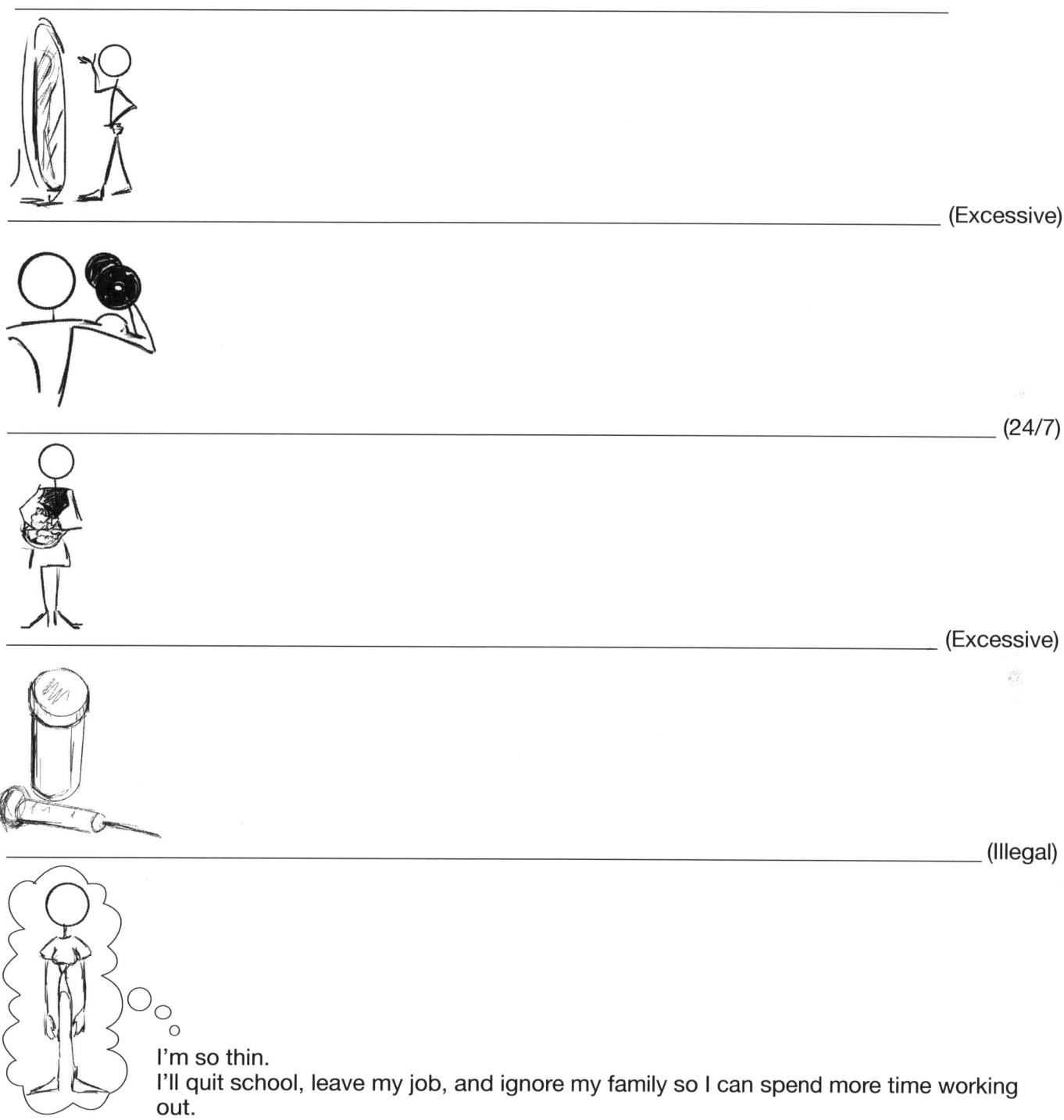

_____ (Excessive)

_____ (24/7)

_____ (Excessive)

_____ (Illegal)

I'm so thin.
I'll quit school, leave my job, and ignore my family so I can spend more time working out.

If you think you might have these warning signs, talk with a parent or caregiver, physician, therapist, dietician and/or coach who is familiar with this condition.

TEENS – Body Image and Beyond

Mirrors and Muscles
FOR THE FACILITATOR

I. Purpose
To identify possible signs of Muscle Dysmorphia and seek help.

II. General Comments
Both genders are susceptible to the Muscle Dysmorphia. Other terms for the condition are *bigorexia* and *reverse anorexia nervosa*. Teens with normal weight and musculature see skinny images in the mirror. They are obsessed with the idea that they are not muscular enough and compare themselves with an unattainable ideal. Athletes are particularly susceptible due to the pressure to be muscular. TV ads focus on *six-packs*. Feelings of depression and disgust often result.

III. Possible Activities
a. Write on the board *Mirror, mirror on the wall…*
b. Ask teens to yell out possible completions (who is fairest, most muscular, etc.).
c. Encourage a discussion regarding how people see distorted images of themselves.
d. Distribute the *Mirrors and Muscles* handout and allow time for completion.
e. Pictures portray constant self-examination, excessive body building or exercise, eating several huge high protein meals daily and getting upset if a meal is missed, taking anabolic steroids, neglecting job, relationships and responsibilities to have time for work outs, delusions of being underweight and having poor musculature.
f. Encourage teens to acknowledge signs or symptoms and speak to a parent, teacher, coach, spiritual advisor, or health care professional.

IV. Enrichment Activities
a. **How much is too much?** Discuss that it is quite normal to check the mirror, try to eat healthy to include all basic nutrients, and exercise; however, these become excessive when teens obsess, ignore other aspects of life, and focus completely on body building. Delusions and distortions that an average (or above) body is underweight with poor musculature is another indicator.

b. **The Female Athlete Triad** may be discussed. Teens who are trying to be thin for gymnastics or other light weight sports are at risk. List the symptoms and discuss:
- Disordered eating, from avoiding certain foods to a full-fledged eating disorder.
- Amenorrhea, loss of menses or irregular periods due to excess exercise and limited nutrition.
- Osteoporosis, decreased calcium, lower bone density and risks for fractures.

Encourage awareness that the teen, along with her school nurse or counselor, physician, therapist, nutritionist astute in this issue, and coach all need to coordinate their efforts.

Shape, Size and Sports

What is Sportsmanship?

Sportsmanship isn't just about shaking hands after the game. It's about the spirit of competition dealing with adversity and handling authority. It is about teammates and opponents treating each other with respect and appreciation. It is about winning OR losing with dignity.

Tell how you have either demonstrated or ignored these slogans regarding sportsmanship:

Play by the rules. _____

Be a humble winner. _____

Be a good loser. _____

Compliment the competition. _____

Share the glory. _____

Don't play the blame game. _____

Learn from mistakes. _____

Challenge yourself. _____

Accept decisions. _____

Play for the fun of it. _____

Apply these quotations to you:

You measure a player from the head up. ~ Al McGuire

The man who has no imagination has no wings. ~ Mohammed Ali

Sportsmanship is more than just for sports. It represents characteristics you need for life.

~ Joseph Dritch, teenager

TEENS – Body Image and Beyond

What is Sportsmanship?

FOR THE FACILITATOR

I. Purpose
To consider character building in sports and reinforce sportsmanship.

II. General Comments
Teens need to value winning mind-sets. They will apply slogans and quotations to their lives by personalizing sportsmanship slogans and quotations and by playing a game, (optional).

III. Possible Activities
1. Individual Activity
   Distribute the *What is Sportsmanship?* handout and ask teens to respond to the slogans and quotations in writing and/or share their ideas aloud.
2. Sportsmanship Game
   a. Ask a volunteer to draw a stick figure on the board with:
      - Head, eyes, nose, mouth, and ears
      - Body
      - Arms
      - Legs
      - Hands with five fingers each
      - Upper arm and thigh muscles
   b. Explain that this is how they will draw the body when it is their turn.
   c. Write *Body or mind?* on the board.
   d. Briefly elicit teens' ideas regarding physical fitness as well as mental attitudes in sports.
   e. Explain they will complete the handout, then use the phrases in the game.
   f. Distribute the *What is Sportsmanship?* handout and allow time for completion.
   g. Tell teens to take a good look at the slogans and quotes and try to remember them.
   h. Teens turn over their completed handouts, blank side up; *contestants* may not see the slogans.
   i. To play the game:
      - Teens take turns taking their handouts to the board, and selecting a sentence.
      - They put blank lines on the board for each letter; spaces between words.
      - Audience (contestants) take turns guessing letters as the volunteer prints them on the lines.
      - Incorrect letters are listed at the bottom of the board.
      - For each incorrect letter, a body part is drawn, as in "a" above.
      - The teen who correctly guesses the sentence shares how he or she has demonstrated or ignored the slogan or personalizes the quote.
      - If he/she wishes, the correct guesser may read the response from his/her handout.
      - The correct guesser erases the board and selects the next sentence.
      - If no one guesses correctly by the time the stick figure is complete, the volunteer reveals the sentence and another volunteer goes to the board.

IV. Enrichment Activities
Encourage teens to compose their own slogans or words of wisdom or to share mottos or jingles they have heard.

A DIFFERENT ⑤ PERSPECTIVE

Most of the shadows of life are caused by standing in our own sunshine.
— RALPH WALDO EMERSON

What's My Secret? .... page 53 ▶
Teens personify distortions and eating disorders; peers guess their identities; sources of help are discussed.

Who Is On My Team? .... page 55 ▶
Teens identify helpful professionals and link their expertise with the treatment of various disorders.

Emotional Overeating: Are you a Tortoise or a Hare? .... page 57 ▶
Through a team game, teens differentiate between winning and defeating ideas; they recognize the possible love-hate relationship with food and brainstorm ways to get a high from life.

SCRATCH THE SURFACE .... page 59 ▶
Teens uncover underlying emotions and issues and realize it's not about food, flaws, weight or muscles.

Ace the Quiz .... page 61 ▶
Teens contemplate alternatives to food-fixes and identify stress reduction skills; they compare fleeting, false comforts to enduring self-soothing techniques.

Cut Out Cutting .... page 63 ▶
Teens identify issues related to self-mutilation and practice expressing emotions with words, symbols, scribbles and drawing.

Disarm Disability .... page 65 ▶
Teens consider a role model who overcame obstacles and found his/her purpose in life; teens with challenging conditions learn they are not alone; other teens recognize that people with disabilities are more like them than they are different.

What's My Secret?

1. I check my mirror almost constantly; I obsess about flaws that others don't see. I avoid people; they would just stare at me, thinking I'm ugly. Plastic surgery fixed a fault but now a new imperfection is ruining my life.

    What's my secret?

2. People say I am underweight but I feel plump and fear fat. I put myself on a strict diet and strenuous exercise plan. I can't be with friends because they're always eating pizza and chips. I'm cold, tired, and depressed.

    What's my secret?

3. I eat huge amounts, make myself throw up and use laxatives. If I'm with people and overeat, I find excuses to use the bathroom, and turn on faucets so they don't hear me. I am getting chipmunk cheeks from enlarged salivary glands and my teeth are decaying from stomach acids.

    What's my secret?

4. I eat several times a day, mostly protein to help me bulk up. I work out a lot and quit my job to have more time for body building. I can't be bothered by family or friends. People say I am athletic and muscular but I see myself as too thin. I am tempted to try steroids and growth hormones.

    What's my secret?

5. I gorge myself with food frequently but am afraid to take laxatives and cannot make myself vomit. I like to eat alone so people don't see how much I consume. I keep gaining weight but can't stop packing in the food.

    What's my secret?

TEENS – Body Image and Beyond

What's My Secret?

FOR THE FACILITATOR

I. Purpose
To identify some indications of eating disorders and image issues.

To help teens who potentially have the problem(s) to know they are not alone.

II. General Comments
Puberty's changes, media and social influences contribute to teen obsessions with weight, appearance and acceptance. Eating disorders and image distortions may result. (The feelings underlying these conditions are addressed in the session, the *Scratch the Surface* handout).

III. Possible Activities
a. Before session:
- Cut the reproducible page into sections as indicated by the lines.
- Ask for five volunteers who are comfortable reading aloud.
- Give each volunteer a description. Privately tell each teen the secret they will be describing before they read it.
- Secret descriptions correspond to the numbers below.
  1. Body Dysmorphic Disorder
  2. Anorexia Nervosa
  3. Bulimia
  4. Muscle Dysmorphia
  5. Binge Eating Disorder

b. During session, volunteers sit at the front of the room.
- To enhance the challenge, do not write the disorders on the board; (to make it easier, write the disorders in random order on the board).
- Volunteers read descriptions; the audience guesses their secrets.
- As peers guess correctly, write the disorder, (or circle it if the disorder was previously written) on the board.

c. Alternative: The disorders are not revealed on the page so facilitators may:
- Distribute the reproducible page, uncut.
- Encourage teens to guess and write each disorder.
- Encourage a discussion of their answers.

IV. Enrichment Activities
a. Teens role play a scenario where two teens eat together, one runs to the bathroom, one follows and realizes the friend is vomiting. The bulimic teen tries to swear the peer to secrecy. What does the friend do? (Ideally the teen encourages peer to tell a parent, school nurse or counselor). The audience gives feedback to the players.

b. List on the board and discuss types of help available: medical treatment to check nutritional and medication needs; individual therapy to uncover underlying issues; family counseling to address dynamics and help parents understand teen problems; group therapy and support groups to help teens learn from each other and process similar issues.

A Different Perspective ▶

Who Is On My Team?

1. I might be the first adult you tell. I may not be able to help with your issues but will recommend people who totally understand.

    Who Am I?

2. I am interested in electrolytes in your body like sodium and potassium. I know if you are anemic or dehydrated and I may prescribe vitamins, minerals and medicine for your physical health.

    Who Am I?

3. I have a license to practice medicine and specialize in mental disorders. I may prescribe medications like anti-depressants.

    Who am I?

4. I help athletes build muscle and improve their performance through diet. I work closely with coaches and trainers to match your intake with your activity level.

    Who am I?

5. With me you will do talk therapy. You talk mostly; I listen and help you identify issues, cope and problem solve. You call me doctor, but I do not prescribe medications.

    Who am I?

6. I work a lot with couples and families. I can help your parents understand; I focus on family dynamics and conflict resolution; I also provide individual therapy.

    Who am I?

7. I help with every day problems like finding resources for food and shelter. I also provide mental health therapy for individuals and families.

    Who am I?

8. I specialize in food and nutrition to help you lead a healthy lifestyle and achieve health-related goals.

    Who Am I?

9. I am the most important team member. I have to work hard and be open to teammates' ideas. They alone cannot fix the problems but with my cooperation we will succeed.

    Who Am I?

TEENS – Body Image and Beyond

Who Is On My Team?

FOR THE FACILITATOR

I. Purpose
To identify the people who may help teens recover from disorders and distortions.

II. General Comments
Teens need to ask trusted adults for assistance and know the kinds of helpers available.

III. Possible Activities
a. Before session:
- Cut the reproducible page into sections as indicated by the lines.
- Ask for nine volunteers who are comfortable reading aloud.
- Each gets a description. Privately tell each teen the identity they will be describing before they read it.
- Encourage volunteers to guess and note their identities.
- The answer key below coincides with the numbers on the descriptions:
  1. Parent, relative, teacher, counselor, school nurse, coach, or religious leader
  2. Physician
  3. Psychiatrist
  4. Sports Nutritionist
  5. Psychologist
  6. Therapist, Counselor, Social Worker
  7. Social Worker or Therapist
  8. Dietitian
  9. Me

b. During session, volunteers sit at the front of the room.
- To enhance the challenge, do not write identities on the board; (or to make it easier, write the identities in random order on the board).
- Volunteers read descriptions; the audience guesses their identities.

c. Instruct teens with descriptions to write their identities in the backs of their slips of paper, then tape the identity label to their shirts for audience to see.

d. Write the following on the board:
- Body Dysmorphic Disorder (imagining or exaggerating flaws)
- Anorexia Nervosa (starving and exercising excessively)
- Bulimia (eating large amounts then purging)
- Muscle Dysmorphia (building muscles obsessively, eating and working out too much)
- Binge Eating Disorder (eating huge amounts but no purging)

e. Audience teens take turns stating one of the disorders and identifying who they would want on their treatment team and why. (No right or wrong answers; teens justify their responses and receive feedback).

IV. Enrichment Activities
Encourage teens to discuss whether and why they might study to become one of the professionals; address the challenges and rewards of these occupations.

A Different Perspective

Emotional Overeating: Are you a Tortoise or a Hare?

Remember Aesop's Fable where the slow but steady tortoise won and the hasty hare lost? Winning the war against emotional overeating is similar. There are no quick fixes; gradual changes work.

For each statement below, write a "T" for tortoise, (*winning idea*) or an "H" for hare, (*defeating idea*).

1. _____ Diets and willpower work.

2. _____ It's all about being hungry and eating food.

3. _____ Emotions like depression and anxiety trigger binges.

4. _____ Guilt from overeating brings on more cravings.

5. _____ Stop sugar, starch, and junk foods immediately.

6. _____ Decrease unhealthy foods a little at a time.

7. _____ Food and food-thoughts are positive distractions for upsetting situations.

8. _____ When under stress, comfort-food has staying power.

9. _____ Change your thoughts to change your feelings and actions.

10. _____ Binge eaters benefit from better ways to handle emotions.

11. _____ Keep your eye on the prize – the perfect weight.

12. _____ Beat up on yourself if you blow your diet.

13. _____ Therapy to deal with real problems takes too long.

14. _____ Support groups for overeaters make you hungrier.

15. _____ Order a large pizza but try to eat only one slice.

16. _____ Order a personal size pizza and plan to eat it all.

17. _____ Have a list of people to call when cravings come.

18. _____ Have an accountability buddy with whom to discuss problems and progress.

19. _____ A list of coping skills is useless when it comes to eating.

20. _____ Think about how great you'll feel if you MMM (*Manage Moods without Munching*).

TEENS – Body Image and Beyond

Emotional Overeating: Are you a Tortoise or a Hare?

FOR THE FACILITATOR

I. Purpose

To understand there is no magic "diet" or "miracle potion" and that emotions drive eating (in food addictions).

II. General Comments

Obsessing about food distracts from focusing on feelings and situations.

III. Possible Activities

a. Write on the board *Love-Hate* and ask teens to describe love-hate relationships.

b. Encourage a discussion about love-hate relationships with food. Concepts include: excessive carbohydrates elevate blood sugar and mood, then both drop, followed by remorse, weight gain, etc. Teens crave certain unhealthy foods and then are unhappy with what that same food does to their bodies.

c. Ask teens why some people compulsively overeat and obsess about food. Concepts include: trying to feed emotional needs or divert attention away from unpleasant situations. Identifying underlying issues and using coping skills satisfies emotional hunger and decreases binging.

   1. Game Format
   - A volunteer game show host is given the *Emotional Overeating: Are You a Tortoise or Hare?* handout; peers do not get a copy.
   - Host reads the introduction and instructions aloud.
   - Host reads the statements and teen contestants take turns stating tortoise or hare; they may ask peers for help.
   - Answers, ("T" *tortoise* "H" *hare*), are:

1. H	6. T	11. H	16. T
2. H	7. H	12. H	17. T
3. T	8. H	13. H	18. T
4. T	9. T	14. H	19. H
5. H	10. T	15. H	20. T

   2. Individual or Partner Format
   - Distribute the *Emotional Overeating: Are You a Tortoise or Hare?* handout and allow individuals or pairs time for completion.
   - Encourage teens to share responses and reasons they selected "T" or "H".

IV. Enrichment Activities

a. Write on the board **Life itself is the proper binge.** ~ Julia Child.

b. Encourage teens to interpret and apply the quote to their lives.

c. Ask teens to brainstorm ways to get a high from life that won't be followed by the crash after overeating or other poor eating habits.

d. A volunteer lists teens' ideas on the board. Possibilities include creative endeavors like art, crafts, music, poetry, prose; productive pursuits like gardening, decorating their rooms, part-time jobs; enjoyable diversions like TV, movies, books; intellectual exercises like puzzles, online brain games, learning about a topic of interest; physical activity like walks, sports, dance; altruism like helping younger children or peers with schoolwork, volunteering for charitable organizations.

SCRATCH THE SURFACE

You have probably played *Scratch-Off* games at fast food places or have seen lottery scratchers. Under the surface are numbers or pictures that make you win or lose. Distortions and disorders related to body image are similar. Obsessions about physical problems divert attention away from painful emotions underneath. You win by dealing with the real issues!

Scratch the surface to reveal what's really bothering you.

Surface = People focus on flawed features, food, weight, and muscles to manage underlying feelings and conflicts. Scratch the surface and peel off this layer.
I feel sad about
I feel angry about
I feel anxious about
I feel lonely when
I feel afraid of
I have power struggles with these people
My perfectionism is related to
I have been teased about
I feel guilty about
My self-esteem
Instead of excessively controlling food, weight, and appearance, I really need to get control over

TEENS – Body Image and Beyond

SCRATCH THE SURFACE

FOR THE FACILITATOR

I. Purpose
To uncover emotions underlying body image distortions and eating disorders.

II. General Comments
Teens need to recognize it's not about food, flaws, weight, or muscles.
Obsessing about these takes away energy from real issues.

III. Possible Activities
a. Ask teens what is meant by the tip of the iceberg.
b. Elicit we see people's appearance and behaviors; underneath are feelings and issues.
c. Distribute the *Scratch the Surface* handout and allow time for completion.
d. Encourage teens to share their most insightful responses.

IV. Enrichment Activities

a. Encourage brainstorming as a whole group, or divide into three or four small clusters.

b. Volunteers take turns writing peers' ideas on the board.

c. Causes of eating and image-related disorders:
   - Psychological Situations
   - Interpersonal Situations
   - Cultural Situations
   - Biological and Genetic Situations

d. Possible lists may include:
   - Psychological – feelings of inadequacy, depression, anxiety, anger, loneliness, low self-esteem.
   - Interpersonal – troubled families and relationships, difficulty expressing emotions, target of ridicule for being different, and history of being abused.
   - Cultural – society glamorizes tallness, thinness, athletic builds, and values external versus internal attributes.
   - Biological and Genetic – Eating disorders may run in families; chemical imbalances may affect appetite, feelings of fullness, and emotions such as depression or obsessive-compulsive tendencies.

e. Write on the board: *How to Be Perfectly Miserable*.
   - Encourage a discussion of the perfectionism that drives these disorders.
   Elicit that in addition to wanting the perfect face and body, perfectionistic teens usually seek the best grades, sports performance, clothes, friends, etc.
   Teens often strive for the appearance that all is well with them, but suffer in silence.

A Different Perspective

Ace the Quiz

Game Show Host Instructions
When a team picks a topic read the question only, not the italicized text. Accept any reasonable response. The italicized text provides suggestions which may be read to players after they respond.

Craving Comfort
1. **What are comfort-foods?** *Feel-good foods associated with childhood treats or remedies for illness.*
2. **Give examples of comfort-foods.** *Different for everyone, i.e., chicken soup, macaroni and cheese.*
3. **What emotions may trigger cravings for comfort food?** *Disappointment, rejection, anxiety.*
4. **What happens if you stuff your feelings by stuffing your face?** *Weight gain, regret, only temporary relief.*
5. **Instead of turning to food, what can you do to relieve stress?** *Use stress management and coping skills, seek counseling.*

Soothing Senses
1. **What might you look at to improve your mood and attitude?** *Flowers, trees, TV, videos, photos, art.*
2. **What might you listen to?** *Sounds in nature, wind chimes, music, your own positive affirmations.*
3. **How might the sense of smell help?** *Pine, peppermint, lavender, lemon, cinnamon, eucalyptus, incense, fresh flowers, scented candles.*
4. **How might the sense of touch help?** *Soft blankets, water, warmth, a hug, petting an animal.*
5. **How might the sense of taste help without overeating?** *Herbal tea, hot chocolate.*

Why Not?
1. **Why not seek comfort in popularity or romance?** *May not find it, may be short-lived, disappointing.*
2. **Why not seek comfort in getting the best grades or winning at games?** *May not always succeed.*
3. **Why not seek comfort in money, clothes, cars, electronics?** *Temporary relief, never enough stuff.*
4. **Why not seek comfort in a flawless face and body?** *Unrealistic goal and will not last forever.*
5. **Why not seek comfort in drugs and alcohol?** *Addicting, life threatening, temporary fix.*

Why?
1. **Why seek self-acceptance?** *You have control over your thoughts, not dependence on others.*
2. **Why do your best?** *Comfort in knowing you tried regardless of grades, wins or losses.*
3. **Why treat others as you want to be treated?** *Creates peaceful relationships and feels good.*
4. **Why value your face and physique, flaws and all?** *They're uniquely yours.*
5. **Why comfort yourself with spirituality?** *Hope, faith, calmness, inner-self peace.*

Comfort Cans
1. **How can talking and being assertive help?** *Vent stress, self-preservation and confidence builds strength.*
2. **How can positive self-talk help?** *Calming and confidence-building phrases comfort and motivate.*
3. **How can helping others promote your own comfort?** *Take your mind off yourself, feels good.*
4. **How can exercising help?** *Boosts endorphins, (feel good chemicals), releases nervous energy.*
5. **How can doing what you love help?** *Music, art, writing, etc. give a natural high, decrease stress by using different parts of the brain.*

TEENS – Body Image and Beyond

Ace the Quiz
FOR THE FACILITATOR

I. Purpose
To consider alternatives to over-indulgence with comfort foods.

To differentiate between fleeting external and enduring internal self-soothing techniques.

II. General Comments
Teens learn stress reduction techniques while playing a team game.

Encourage teens to seek professional help if these interventions are ineffective.

III. Possible Activities
a. Ask for a volunteer game show host who is comfortable reading aloud.
b. Ask for a volunteer score-keeper who is comfortable writing on the board.
c. Provide a photocopied *Ace the Quiz* give handout to the host who sits in front of the room.
d. Divide teens into two teams, Number A and Number B; teammates sit near each other to confer.
e. Teams take turns selecting a category, host asks the question, members collaborate and respond.
f. Host accepts any reasonable responses, then reads the text, (possible responses for each question, italicized).
g. Scorekeeper copies the score sheet below onto the board and puts A or B in boxes as teams answer questions.
h. The team to earn the most letters wins.

IV. Enrichment Activities
Encourage teens to keep a stress journal to record stress-inducing triggers, how they reacted and what positive interventions they might have applied instead.

- -

Score-Keeper Instructions: Copy the score sheet onto the board. Place an A or B in each box as teams answer questions. The team to earn the most letters wins.

Craving Comfort	Soothing Senses	Why Not?	Why?	Comfort *Cans*

A Different Perspective

Cut Out Cutting

Some people self-mutilate; they cut, burn, or harm themselves. People often do this to release pain.

Check boxes that apply to you regarding risks:
- ❏ Low self-esteem.
- ❏ History of being emotionally, physically or sexually abused.
- ❏ Taught in childhood to hide emotions, especially anger and sadness.
- ❏ Feel empty inside.
- ❏ An eating disorder (starving, binging, purging).
- ❏ Substance abuse.

People injure themselves for many reasons. Finish each sentence to identify a better way to cope:

a. To release inner pain I can _____

b. To get a high or to feel euphoric I can _____

c. To express anger I can _____

d. To express sadness I can _____

Express yourself in the box below. Write (prose or poetry), or draw, (symbols, scribbles, colors, etc.), to describe what you are feeling.

TEENS – Body Image and Beyond

Cut Out Cutting

FOR THE FACILITATOR

I. Purpose

To help teens acknowledge if they have self-destructive behaviors and realize they are not alone.

To find a healthier way to express feelings; to seek professional help.

II. General Comments

Teens with eating disorders or other emotional problems may self-mutilate. It becomes a body image issue when they have scars, sometimes for a lifetime, that tell the world of their internal pain.

III. Possible Activities

a. Before session recruit an artistic participant and privately coach him or her.
b. At the start of session, the volunteer draws an arm with cut marks.
c. Ask teens, *What happened in this picture?*
   Elicit that the person was cut; elicit that the person did it to himself or herself.
d. Ask teens to brainstorm why people would self mutilate.
e. A volunteer lists their ideas on the board.
f. Distribute the *Cut Out Cutting* handout and allow time for completion.
   Encourage teens to share their responses.
   Possible responses:
   - Talk with someone I trust
   - Exercise
   - Journal
   - Cry – let tears out rather than blood
g. Encourage teens with this issue to acknowledge it after the session by talking to a parent, trusted adult, school counselor or nurse, spiritual or religious leader or their physician.

IV. Enrichment Activities

a. Ask teens to brainstorm components of recovery from self-harm.
b. A volunteer lists their ideas on the board.
c. The list may include but is not limited to:
   - Admit the problem and ask for help.
   - Want to stop; want to learn healthier ways to cope.
   - Medications.
   - Use therapy to discover and treat underlying issues, (anxiety, anger, guilt, elational problems).
   - Use family counseling to help parents and siblings understand and assist.
   - Use trauma therapy if the teen was or is being abused.
   - Use cognitive behavioral therapy to examine how thoughts affect feelings and behavior; to learn to change negative thinking patterns.
   - Use dialectical behavioral therapy to help with regulating emotions and testing reality, (as with cognitive behavioral therapy); to teach distress tolerance, acceptance, and mindful awareness.

Disarm Disability

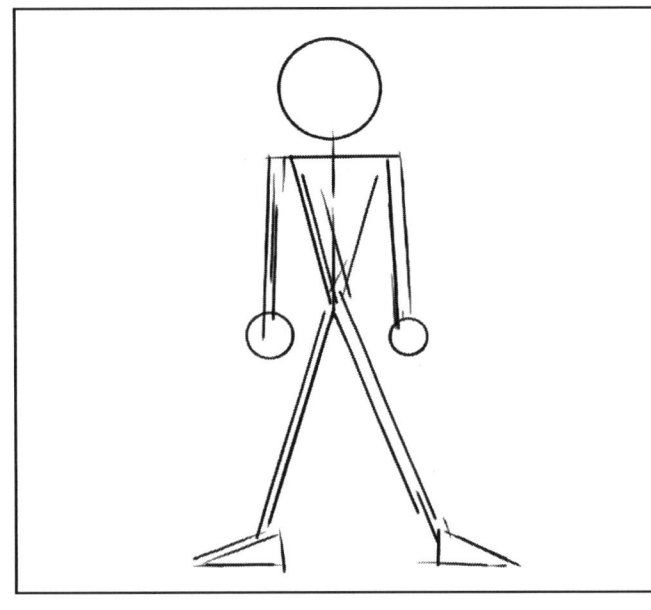

Cross off both arms and both legs on the illustration on the left.

You now see a representation of Nick Vujicic born without limbs, in 1982, in Australia.

In each set below, circle the words that you think described Nick after peers bullied him:

    Low self-esteem   or   high self-esteem

    Loneliness   or   lots of friends

    Depressed   or   happy

    Suicidal   or   life was worth living

What attitudes do you think might have kept him alive and helped him to finish college with a double Bachelor's degree?

_____

_____

_____

_____

_____

_____

_____

Nick founded a non-profit organization, *Life without Limbs*, and discovered his life purpose. Put yourself in Nick's shoes and write a brief talk to inspire and motivate people who feel different or disabled.

_____

_____

_____

_____

_____

_____

_____

TEENS – Body Image and Beyond

Disarm Disability

FOR THE FACILITATOR

I. Purpose
To help teens with body image issues related to differences or disabilities, to discover they are not alone. To inspire physically intact teens to have empathy and be less likely to bully.

To reveal a role model with severe physical deficits whose purpose is to motivate and inspire others.

II. General Comments
Teens with disabilities and disfigurements are at risk for body image issues, especially if shunned by peers. Unfortunately, movies, music videos and mass media rarely show role models with differences. Online videos and DVDs regarding Nick Vujicic and other people who have overcome obstacles help teens believe and achieve.

III. Possible Activities
- Write Hide, Cover, Fix on the board.
- Ask what traits people might try to hide, cover or fix and why. (*Differences, deficits*).
- Distribute *Disarm Disability* and allow time for completion.
- Encourage teens to share their responses.
- To illustrate the value of trusting others, seeking and giving support, encourage teens to take a "trust walk." One leads another person who is blindfolded around the room.

IV. Enrichment Activities
a. Ask teens what they have heard about the Elephant Man.
b. Explain the disorder causes disfiguring tumors, overgrowth of tissues and bones.
c. Explain that actress Gillian Anderson, (X-Files and many other productions), has a brother with the condition and is a spokesperson for NF, (Neurofibromatosis).
d. Ask teens to consider:
   - What disorder, illness or condition is close to your heart and why?
   - If you were a spokesperson for that condition, describe your message.
e. Put the example below on the board and encourage teens to compose a poem (as a group, or individually), from the person's perspective who has a disability:

> *Look at me from afar.*
> *Am I marred? Am I scarred?*
> *Look inside.*
> *I've nothing to hide.*
> *I am more like you,*
> *Than you ever knew.*

f. Put the example below on the board and encourage teens to compose a poem (as a group, or individually), from an onlooker's perspective:

> *I look at you and I see*
> *Who I am afraid to be.*
> *Yet you are so spiritedly,*
> *Adept to empower humanity.*

BODY SIZE 6 DIVERSITY

The gifts of nature are infinite in their variety, and mind differs from mind almost as much as body from body.
— QUINTILIAN

Weight: War and Peace .... page 69 ▶
The benefits of fitness rather than striving to please others are promoted; teens learn that their bodies need not define them.

Spin to Win .... page 71 ▶
Teens twirl their pencils, focus terms and learn concepts related to individual normal weight ranges versus chasing a number on a scale.

Size and Sensitivity .... page 73 ▶
By creating posters, slogans and skits, teens value all shapes and sizes; teens identify ways to engage in charitable efforts.

Body Topics for Blogs and/or Panels .... page 75 ▶
Teens write and/or discuss ideas about controversial concepts including ways to decrease discrimination against people with physical differences and how to feed emotional hunger; ten other topics are addressed.

A Different Perspective

Weight: War and Peace

First Lady Michelle Obama observed an overweight girl convincing her mom to buy potato chips and a sugary, slushy drink. She noted similar situations and launched Let's Move! The program promotes healthier food and more physical activity.

What would you do if you were the mom that Michelle Obama saw?

_____

_____

Circle talk balloons that are true for you. Place an "X" on ones that are false.

- I'll be in the most popular clique if I'm super skinny.
- I want to look, feel, and be my best.
- I'll get the best looking dates if my body is perfect.
- I'll please my best friend.
- I'll have energy to do what I love.
- I might not get high blood pressure.
- I'll keep my partner from cheating if I look better than everyone.
- I need to make peace with my current body.
- I'll reduce my chances of diabetes.
- I'll be the team star or best cheerleader if I'm in peak shape.
- My identity is not my body shape.
- My parents try to force me to change my weight.
- Bullying people makes them lose weight.
- I'll lower my chance of heart disease.
- I'll help prevent diabetes. and heart disease.
- If my friends make fun of someone, I should join in.
- If bullied, I'll use positive self-talk.

I will make peace with my less than perfect body by _____

_____

_____

© 2013 WHOLE PERSON ASSOCIATES, 101 WEST 2ND ST., SUITE 203, DULUTH MN 55802 • 800-247-6789

TEENS – Body Image and Beyond

Weight: War and Peace

FOR THE FACILITATOR

I. Purpose
　　To highlight fitness benefits versus striving for perfection and trying to please others.
　　To help teens accept less than perfect bodies and know their bodies do not define them.

II. General Comments
　　Michelle Obama's *Let's Move!* plan provides information for parents, encourages healthy food at school, improves access and affordability regarding healthy choices, and promotes more exercise. The *Let's Move!* website has a wealth of information and suggestions to tackle and prevent childhood obesity.

III. Possible Activities
　　a. Write *Let's Move!* on the board and elicit what teens know; explain briefly about the program.
　　b. Distribute the *Weight: War and Peace* handout and ask a volunteer to read information at the top.
　　c. Allow time for teens to complete the written portion of the page.
　　d. Encourage teens to share responses; elicit rationales for the false statements. Possibilities:
　　　　• Thinness does not guarantee acceptance into a clique; if it did, would they want those pseudo-friends? Similar ideas apply to (supposedly) the best dates, preventing cheating, pleasing a friend or being a star.
　　　　• Their parents cannot make them do it; healthy choices are theirs in adolescence.
　　　　• Discuss that bullying has caused suicides; teens should deter peers from bullying.
　　e. Encourage teens to discuss the importance of self-acceptance and esteem based on internal attributes; they can love themselves while working toward better nutrition and more activity.

IV. Enrichment Activities
　　Ask teens to brainstorm or discuss the following topics; possible ideas to elicit are provided.
　　a. People who are concerned about weight might help themselves in these ways:
　　　　• Talk to a family member, school counselor, nurse, teacher, therapist or doctor.
　　　　• Express feelings by drawing, painting, journaling, sculpting, writing poetry.
　　　　• Find social settings where interests and abilities matter more than size.
　　　　• Volunteer to help others or animals or get involved in a cause one believes in.
　　　　• Use positive self-talk; be assertive and tell school personnel about verbal abuse.
　　　　• Focus on what would be important if weight were not an issue.
　　b. How might a person burn more calories fairly painlessly?
　　　　• Use TV and computer time as a reward: do a physical sport or exercise first, then relax.
　　　　• Walk, rather than ride, to a bus stop, park or be dropped off a distance from destination.
　　　　• Use stairs instead of elevators or escalators.
　　c. How might a person consume fewer calories fairly painlessly?
　　　　• Increase vegetables, fruits; eat moderate amounts of lean protein and whole grains; low fat foods.
　　　　• Do not skip breakfast or any meal; pack healthy foods for snack attacks.
　　　　• Drink 6-8 glasses of water a day; If you must, dilute soda or juices with half water or club soda.
　　　　• Don't get too hungry, angry, lonely or tired as these conditions and emotions trigger cravings.
　　　　• Do not beat yourself up if you stray from your plan; just get back on track.
　　　　• Allow a splurge once weekly; eat your favorite foods but in smaller portions.
　　　　• When tempted to overeat remember, you will eat again in a few hours.
　　　　• Remind yourself how happy you'll be later if you do not overeat.
　　　　• Find friends or mentors who have sensibly met and maintained a fitness goal.
　　　　• Find veggies at parties, eat fruit while studying; order baked versus fried foods at a restaurant, etc.

A Different Perspective

Spin to Win

**When it is your turn, tell what the term means to you.
You may ask peers for help and feedback.**

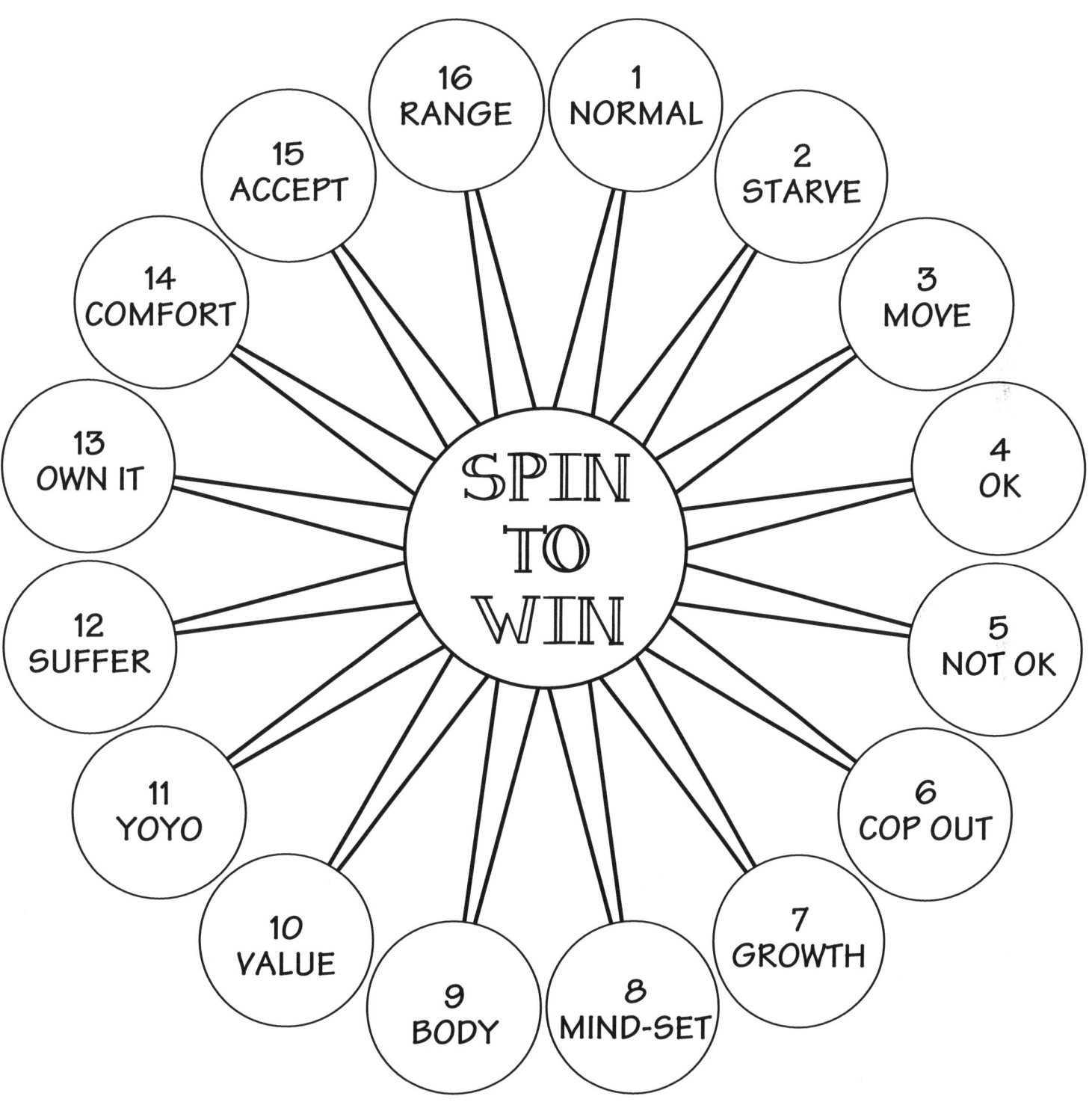

TEENS – Body Image and Beyond

Spin to Win
FOR THE FACILITATOR

I. Purpose
To consider accepting basic body types while promoting healthy lifestyles.

II. General Comments
Ideas about individual "normal" weight ranges are most applicable to older teens, after their growth spurts and as they become adults. This activity helps teens recognize inborn tendencies while maximizing health and fitness as they come within realistic parameters.

III. Possible Activities
1. Spin the Pencil Game Format
   a. Draw a big thermometer on the board. Place a mark at 98.6 F.
   b. Ask what is represented; discuss the body's self-regulated normal temperature and the fact that not everyone's normal temperature is 98.6. Different people have different "normals" regarding temperature, height, body build, etc.
   c. Explain that weight may be similarly regulated at a "normal" range, different for each person.
   d. Distribute the *Spin to Win* handout.
   e. Teens take turns spinning a pencil on the handout until it stops and points to a circled term.
   f. The teen, with peer help if needed, explains the term, receives feedback; there are no rights or wrongs.
   g. After the teen's interpretation, facilitator reads the corresponding explanation below.
   h. The teen then personalizes the concept.
   i. As the game progresses, teens cross off used terms and select the unused term closest to where their pencils point after spinning.

2. Individual Activity
   Teens share interpretations and personalize terms in writing and/or aloud. Peers give feedback.

Ideas to elicit and read after teens give their impressions include:

1. Normal – possibly an internal thermostat regulates weight within a personal "normal" range.
2. Starve – the body senses starvation, increases hunger and food obsessions, slows metabolism.
3. Move – exercise can keep weight at the low end of one's range or may over-ride plump tendencies.
4. OK – some teens are ok with their own "normal," relieved to stop chasing a number on the scale.
5. Not OK – some teens, not ok with their own "normal," succeed at maintaining their chosen weight.
6. Cop-out – some see accepting a natural weight range as a cop out and work toward different goals.
7. Growth – growth spurts in teens usually cause each individual's normal height and weight to increase.
8. Mind-set – a doomed mind-set may sabotage weight loss maintenance; *I'll always be chubby*.
9. Body – genes predispose thin or stocky builds; nutrition and exercise affect weight and fitness.
10. Value – valuing character traits like compassion helps diminish body image concerns.
11. Yo-yo – many get on a cycle of weight loss and gain, emotionally frustrating yo-yo dieting.
12. Suffer – suffering through starvation diets often backfires with binging.
13. Own it – it's your body, you decide what to accept and what to change; celebrate its health.
14. Comfort – be comfortable in your own skin; embrace your heredity and maximize your assets.
15. Accept – self-acceptance is not a number on a scale; it's positive thoughts, supportive relationships.
16. Range – aim to be at your best within a comfortable and maintainable weight or musculature range.

IV. Enrichment Activities
Encourage teens to brainstorm 16 different words or phrases, define and personalize the concepts.

Terms may relate to body image, internal traits, peer pressure, or any topics important to participants.

A Different Perspective ▶

Size and Sensitivity

Size Slogan Team

Your team will brainstorm tee shirt slogans for body size diversity.

Example: Friends are thick and thin.

Size Poster Team

Your team will create a poster(s) promoting body size diversity.

Example: Depict short, tall, slim and heavy people exercising with caption:

"Fitness comes in all sizes."

Size Video Team

Your team will rehearse a brief skit promoting body size diversity.

Example: Two teens bully a thin student; a well-liked classmate asks the person being bullied to go out.

Sensitivity Slogan Team

Your team will brainstorm humanitarian efforts you might launch.

Example: Help a charitable organization that collects used eyeglasses for people who need them.

Sensitivity Poster Team

Your team will create a poster promoting teens who help others.

Example: Depict teens coaching kids with disabilities in sports.

Sensitivity Video Team

Your team will rehearse a brief skit illustrating teens helping others.

Example: Dating abuse occurs, (yelling, pretend hitting); a witness calls 911 and informs the audience about abuse prevention.

TEENS – Body Image and Beyond

Size and Sensitivity
FOR THE FACILITATOR

I. Purpose
To value people of all sizes and shapes and to encourage a variety of humanitarian efforts.

II. General Comments
Teens will view body size diversity in a non-judgmental manner and consider different ways to help others. As altruism increases, body image issues are de-emphasized.

III. Possible Activities
a. Before session, cut the *Size and Sensitivity* handout on the dotted lines.
b. Provide lined paper for the slogan teams and crayons, markers and large paper for the poster teams. Additionally supply clay to sculpt, and magazines, (cut-outs for collages), with tape or glue.
c. Write on the board *Body size diversity* and *Humanitarianism*.
d. Encourage a discussion of social actions that embrace people of all sizes and shapes like *Big is Beautiful* with plus size models, and *Health at Every Size* promoting peace with your body and food.
e. Discuss teen humanitarians who tutor or coach younger kids or help elderly neighbors, etc.
f. Write on the board the six team options that are listed on the handout.
g. Allow teens to choose but encourage a fairly even number of teens among the teams.
h. Allow team members to sit in clusters and the video team to practice away from others.
i. Distribute the cut-out instructions from the *Size and Sensitivity* handout to the corresponding teams and allow time to write, draw or rehearse.
j. Teens re-convene; slogans and posters are shared with the group and feedback is shared.
k. Mock videos are performed and feedback is shared.

IV. Enrichment Activity - Relate the following inspirational information to the teens:
a. *CNN Heroes*, http://www.cnn.com/SPECIALS/cnn.heroes/index.html (mostly adults), in the year 2012, and Channel ABC7/KABC-TV in Los Angeles, Cool Kids, http://abclocal.go.com/kabc/channel?section=resources/lifestyle_community/kids&id=7100512 in 2012, honored young people who helped the community. 2012 CNN Heroes included a rape survivor who comforts and counsels victims, a man who provides sporting opportunities for recovering addicts, a woman who supports youth who care for an ill, aged, or disabled family member, a parent whose son drowned who now ensures that other kids learn to swim, etc.

b. 2012 KABC *Cool Kids* included the examples on the handout.
A few of the many stories are about kids who:
- Help youngsters improve reading, writing, mathematics
- Promote anti-bullying campaigns
- Help homeless people with music education
- Help horses have a better life
- Raise awareness of issues like domestic violence, epilepsy, etc.
- Knit to warm cancer patients; make pajamas for kids in need
- Deliver meals in the community

A Different Perspective

Body Topics for Blogs and/or Panels

The topics below have no right or wrong responses. Substantiate your opinion, giving real-life examples if possible.

Options:

1. What does *Body Acceptance* mean to you? Is it a realistic goal for high school and college-age people? Why or Why not?

2. What are the health risks of being underweight? Overweight? What is your opinion about promoting *Health at Any Size*? How might it affect people's physical health and mental health?

3. People have said *you can never be too rich or too thin*. Share whether you agree or disagree and why. Discuss celebrities with good looks and bad behavior and plain lookers who achieve fame and respect.

4. How might a person who is unusually thin, heavy, short or tall, combat negative stereotypes or bullying? Give examples of assertive words and actions, and positive self-talk.

5. What is your opinion of people using diet pills, weight gain formulas, and medical or surgical procedures to alter their shapes? Discuss physical aspects and emotional aspects.

6. In what ways can society decrease discrimination toward people who differ, and embrace body size diversity? What ideas would be included in pamphlets, articles, posters, and public service announcements?

7. Should high schools allow physical education or health teachers or school nurses to weigh students and measure their heights? Why or why not? What can schools do to reward internal attributes?

8. What is your opinion of naturally thin or purposely underweight people, extremely thin, (due to excessive diet and exercise), degrading people in real life (and those who appear in commercials) who eat unhealthy foods?

9. How might TV series, soap operas, music videos, movies, commercials, reality shows, books and other sources of entertainment promote body size diversity?

10. Discuss your experiences with emotional hunger. How does it differ from physical hunger and how do you feed it without food?

11. What can teens do in school and in the community to make their opinions known on other topics important to them via writing, speaking, panels and other forums?

12. Address your own mind-boggling body image issue!

Body Blogs Writing Page

Blogger's Name _____   **Topic Number** _____

Post Your Blog

_____
_____
_____
_____
_____
_____
_____

Reader's Comments   Name _____

_____
_____
_____
_____
_____
_____
_____

Reader's Comments   Name _____

_____
_____
_____
_____
_____
_____
_____

Reader's Comments   Name _____

_____
_____
_____
_____
_____
_____
_____

A Different Perspective

Body Panels Preparation Page

Moderator's Name _____ **Topic Number** _____

Moderator's Introduction Notes

_____
_____
_____
_____
_____
_____
_____

Panelist's Name _____ Panelist's Notes:

_____
_____
_____
_____
_____
_____

Panelist's Name _____ Panelist's Notes:

_____
_____
_____
_____
_____
_____

Panelist's Name _____ Panelist's Notes:

_____
_____
_____
_____
_____
_____

TEENS – Body Image and Beyond

Body Topics for Blogs and/or Panels
FOR THE FACILITATOR

I. Purpose
To explore and exchange ideas about body size diversity; to promote critical thinking. To consider, agree, or respectfully disagree, with peers' opinions.

II. General Comments
Teens will think for themselves, consider others' viewpoints and write blogs or articulate opinions during panel discussions.

III. Possible Activities
1. **Team Blogs**
   a. Ask teens to share their blogging or opinion-writing experiences.
   b. Explain that team members write blogs or instagrams, and may agree or disagree.
   c. Distribute handouts, *Body Topics for Blogs and/or Panels* and *Body Blogs Writing Page*.
   d. Allow teens to pick topics and sit near peers who choose the same topic.
   e. In each team, teens decide who writes the initial blog; others write reader's comments.
   f. Bloggers and readers write on the lines provided; on one page, or their own pages.
   g. The group reunites; teams take turns sitting at the front of the room.
   h. Bloggers and readers read their blogs; peers provide additional views.
   i. Depending on your session's length, limit the blogging and sharing times so all teens write and share; or plan to complete the activity during the next session.

2. **Individual Blogs**

   Teens write blogs about their chosen topics, then share aloud and receive peer feedback.

3. **Panel Discussions**
   a. Ask teens to share experiences watching panel discussions on TV or being on panels.
   b. Explain that team members are panelists and may agree or have different opinions.
   c. Distribute handouts, *Body Topics…* and *Body Panels Preparation Page*.
   d. Allow teens to select topics and sit near peers who chose the same topic.
   e. In each team, teens decide who acts as moderator; others are panelists.
   f. Panelists decide aspects each will address; they should not rehearse but may make notes.
   g. The group reunites; panels take turns sitting at the front of the room and discussing their topics; peers provide additional views.
   h. Depending on your session's time, limit speaking times for each panelist so all teens are able to talk; or plan to complete the activity during the next session.

4. **Combine Body Blogs and Panels**

   All teens receive *Body Topics for Blogs and/or Panels* handout; teens select topics and sit near peers who chose he same topic. Each team decides whether to write blogs or to conduct a panel discussion; each team receives the *Body Blogs Writing Page* or the *Body Panels Preparation Page* depending on their choice. They work together briefly as described in Team Blogs and Panel Discussions (above). When the group reunites, teens either share their blogs or conduct panel discussions and receive peer feedback.

IV. Enrichment Activities
a. Encourage a discussion regarding whether and why their opinions would be different if anonymous, rather than when their identities are known, as in this exercise.
b. Ask teens to share a new idea or viewpoint they heard today.
c. Ask teens to brainstorm topics for future blogs and/or panels to address; the same format can be used in other sessions.

ARE YOU WHAT YOU EAT? 7

Food is the most primitive form of comfort.
— Sheilah Graham

Agree? or Disagree? .... page 81 ▶
Teens take a stand under Agree or Disagree signs and defend their views on eating, exercise, appearance and other topics.

Habits Make Us .... page 83 ▶
Teens note current physical and emotional healthy and not healthy habits; they identify healthy habits they wish to adopt.

Starve, Stuff or Solve? .... page 85 ▶
Teens read and write scenarios or role play ways to integrate healthy eating with socializing.

Create Your Own .... page 87 ▶
Teens create lyrics, limericks, music or poems to describe food-related issues involving family and friends.

Food Fact Jeopardy .... page 89 ▶
Teens play a question and answer game about food's value, facts and fiction; and identify emotional and physical hunger.

Are You What You Eat?

Agree? or Disagree?

Models have the perfect body.	There should be a high soda pop tax.	Restaurants should eliminate jumbo meals.	Extra large sugary drinks should be banned.	Kids' meals with toys should have only healthy foods.
You are what you eat.	You live to eat.	You eat to live.	Crash diets work.	People's appearance tells their autobiography.
Teen beauty pageants build confidence.	The thinner you are the more attractive you are.	A muscular body makes a person appealing.	What people eat is their own business.	Schools should serve only healthy lunches.
Fit is the opposite of fat.	Exercise is a drag!	Appearance determines success.	Physical education should be cut to help the school budget.	People are completely pre-destined by their genes.
It costs a lot of money to be at your peak.	Eating disorders aren't a big deal.	Obesity is caused by uncontrolled eating.	Commercials often give mixed messages.	To be overweight is to be a failure.
Healthy food doesn't taste as good.	"Losing weight" are dirty words.	Exercise helps upset or angry emotions.	Binging does not lead to an eating disorder.	Quick weight loss can easily be maintained.

TEENS – Body Image and Beyond

Agree? or Disagree?
FOR THE FACILITATOR

I. Purpose
To consider controversies in school and society regarding diet, fitness and appearance.

To encourage teens to assertively take a stand and defend their positions.

II. General Comments
Society is attempting to encourage healthy lifestyles. Teens may agree or disagree with the trends; some teens go to extremes. The game helps teens weigh the pros and cons.

III. Possible Activities
1. **Game Format**
   a. Before session, cut the *Diet Disagreements* handout on the dashed lines.
   b. Place cut-outs in a container.
   c. Tape a sheet of paper labeled, **AGREE** on one wall and a sheet of paper labeled **DISAGREE** on the opposite wall.
   d. If possible move chairs away from walls so teens can stand under the signs, or line the walls with chairs for teens to sit under the signs.
   e. When session begins, tell teens they will take turns picking up slips of paper and reading the statements aloud.
   f. When a statement is read, peers will move to the wall labeled AGREE or DISAGREE depending on their opinions.
   g. Explain there are no right or wrong answers, but teens are to substantiate their positions.
   h. Some teens may be *on the fence*, able to see both sides of an issue; they still should decide on the preponderance of evidence, as they see it, and move to the AGREE or DISGAREE wall; when defending their positions they may elaborate about their ambivalence.
   i. After peers take their places, the teen who selected the statement calls on people to defend their views.
   j. The next teen picks and reads a statement; peers move under the signs and share reasons.
   k. Discourage debates back and forth during the game; if a *hot topic* arises, save the debate for later or for another session.
2. **Individual Activity** – Use the uncut page as a handout and instruct teens to write an *A* for *AGREE* or *D* for *DISAGREE* in each box and elaborate on the back of the page. Encourage teens to share their opinions.

IV. Enrichment Activities
a. After the above game, encourage debates on particularly controversial topics.
b. Alternately, teens with the same opinions may meet briefly as teams, list their reasons for agreeing or disagreeing, then debate the teams with the opposing views.
c. Ask teens to compose their own statements; peers then agree or disagree and substantiate their stances.

Are You What You Eat?

Habits Make Us

We first make our habits then our habits make us.
~ John Dryden

List your current physical and emotional health habits in the top boxes and then add ones you hope to adopt below.

My CURRENT Physical Healthy or Not Healthy Habits	My CURRENT Emotional Healthy or Not Healthy Habits
Examples: I eat two fairly healthy meals but skip breakfast. I exercise twice weekly.	*Examples:* I try to think positively but beat up on myself a lot. I compare myself to others.
My FUTURE Physical Healthy Habits I Wish to Adopt	**My FUTURE Emotional Healthy Habits I Wish to Adopt**
Examples: I'll eat a balanced breakfast daily. I'll exercise or participate in sports at least four times a week.	*Examples:* I'll write five positive affirmations daily. I'll be my best self, and be glad I am unique.

TEENS – Body Image and Beyond

Habits Make Us

FOR THE FACILITATOR

I. **Purpose**
   To consider nutrition, exercise, thought patterns and other habits that make a big difference in life.

II. **General Comments**
   Teens look at current habits and plan for improvements.

III. **Possible Activities**
   a. Write the John Dryden quote on the board: *We first make our habits and then our habits make us.*
   b. Ask teens how this quotation relates to eating patterns.
      Elicit that over time, foods and activity levels affect appearance, health, energy, etc.
   c. Ask teens about other habits that can make or break them.
      Elicit ideas. Include the following:
      - Positive - negative thinking.
      - Being with helpful or hurtful friends.
      - Clean and sober lifestyle or drinking and drugs.
      - Honesty or dishonesty.
      - Kindness or cruelty.
      - Diligent study habits or undisciplined study habits.
   d. Explain that the first step is to identify our habits, see how these habits affect us, and decide whether we need to make some changes.
   e. Distribute the *Habits Make Us* handout and allow time for completion.
   f. Encourage teens to share their responses.

IV. **Enrichment Activities**
   a. Ask teens to brainstorm ways to improve nutrition, as a whole group or in teams.
   b. Ask for a volunteer to record their responses on the board or paper. Elicit responses:
      - Increase fresh vegetables; eat fruit rather than drink fruit juice.
      - Eat whole grains, lean meat, poultry, fish, eggs and soy products for protein.
      - Drink non-fat or low-fat milk; eat low-fat dairy products.
      - Drink 6-8 glasses of water a day.
      - Avoid caffeinated and sugary drinks; energy drinks with stimulants can be dangerous.
      - Sports drinks may help replace fluids, carbohydrates and salt.
      - Minimize saturated and trans fats; use olive oil or vegetable oil.
      - Do not skip meals, especially breakfast.
      - Limit junk food, fried food and empty calories in candies, rich desserts, etc.
      - Choose healthy fast food options.
      - In lieu of ice cream, choose frozen yogurt, Italian ices, gelato and fresh fruit for treats.
   c. Encourage teens to discuss how habitual responses to stress can be productive or detrimental. (If done in teams, one lists productive and the other lists detrimental responses). Ideas:
      - Use stress as a motivator for change, rather than falling into self-hatred or self-pity.
      - Face, rather than run from or deny problems, to strengthen coping skills.
      - Take responsibility when warranted, rather than blame others, to develop insight.
      - Express, rather than stuff feelings, to release pent up emotions.
      - Seek trustworthy people or professionals, rather than refusing or not asking for help.

Are You What You Eat?

Starve, Stuff or Solve?

Consider the scenarios and how you would feel if you starved, stuffed, or solved the problems.

Example:

Situation	My dream date wants pizza with pepperoni, sausage, bacon and beef.
Starve	Say, I'm not hungry, and don't eat; drool as my date delves into the pizza.
How would I feel?	Deprived, frustrated, and I might go home and raid the fridge.
Stuff	Chow down on my half; doesn't a hearty appetite help romance?
How would I feel?	Disappointed in myself that I did not stick to my eating plan.
Solve	Suggest ordering my part of the pizza with plain cheese or veggies.
How would I feel?	Satisfied with the food, proud that I made healthy choices.

Fill in the blanks of *How would I feel?* in this scenario:

Situation	My friends want to go out for shakes, burgers and fries.
Starve	Stay home, tell myself, *Ditch fast food junkies; find fitness fanatic friends.*
How would I feel?	
Stuff	Eat what they eat; I don't want to seem like a food snob.
How would I feel?	
Solve	Order a healthy option, a grilled meat sandwich or salad.
How would I feel?	

Now write your own scenario:

Situation	
Starve	
How would I feel?	
Stuff	
How would I feel?	
Solve	
How would I feel?	

TEENS – Body Image and Beyond

Starve, Stuff or Solve?

FOR THE FACILITATOR

I. Purpose

To coordinate social life with healthy nutrition.

To plan ahead to find *middle of the road* solutions versus isolation or succumbing to peer pressure.

II. General Comments

Nutrition conscious teens face dilemmas when peers are not food savvy; or if friends can eat calorie laden foods without weight gain. Teens need not sacrifice socializing while monitoring their intake.

III. Possible Activities

a. Ask teens what they did the last time they were out with friends.

b. Ask about their most recent holiday with family. What did they do? Elicit the common theme of mingling and munching.

c. Distribute the *Starve, Stuff or Solve?* handout.

d. Ask teens to take turns reading the example aloud.

e. Allow time for written completion of the pre-set "How I would feel" scenario and the "Write your own" scenario.

f. Encourage teens to share their responses.

IV. Enrichment Activities

a. Role Plays

- Instead of sharing the scenarios they wrote, they role play.
- They break into teams of at least three teens, and sit in clusters.
- Teens share the scenarios they wrote with their team members.
- They discuss and rehearse their scenarios; one teen is narrator.
- The narrator will ask the audience, (other peers), *How would you feel?* (in places where the handout says *How would I feel?*)
- The whole group reconvenes; teams take turns playing their parts.
- The audience shares how they would feel in the starving, stuffing and solving situations.

b. Encourage a discussion about the opposite circumstance.

- Ask how teens handle eating around diet-obsessed friends at a restaurant or party.
- Do they alter their food choices to fit in, or *dig in* while others diet? Why?
- How do they handle people who advise them to diet if they are not yet ready or willing to change their eating habits?

Are You What You Eat?

Create Your Own...

Try your hand at any type of music, your own lyrics to an existing tune, your own lyrics and music; a poem. These do not need to rhyme. Poems can be serious or humorous.

Relate these creativities to social settings and trying to eat healthfully; or the opposite, to situations where people urge you to diet when you are not ready or willing to eat differently.

For limericks remember – the first two lines rhyme with each other, the second two lines rhyme with each other, and the last line rhymes with the first two. See the AABBA pattern below:

Two Limerick Examples

There once was a guy with some **friends** (A)
Who did not want the friendships to **end** (A)
    But when they pigged **out** (B)
    He wanted to **shout** (B)
"You're setting a terrible **trend**!" (A)

There once were some teens with strict parents
That criticized them without limits.
    When they ate fattening fare
    Families glared and would swear,
"You're gaining more weight by the minute."

TEENS – Body Image and Beyond

Create Your Own...

FOR THE FACILITATOR

I. Purpose
To consider humorous aspects of social settings and healthy choices.

To express frustration or other emotions through lyrics, for any type of music.

II. General Comments
From funerals to festivities, get-togethers involve food. Teens can be food savvy without sacrificing socializing. Teens with weight issues may need to be assertive with people who ridicule or hound them about eating habits.

III. Possible Activities
a. Write *Food, friends and family* on the board and ask teens about the connection. Elicit that relationships, social gatherings and family dynamics often incorporate food.

b. Ask teens to share social situations where something humorous or awkward associated with foods occurred, like being served a disliked food at a friend's house or being reluctant to try a different ethnic dish, etc.

c. Distribute the *Create Your Own . . .* handout; teens take turns reading aloud.

d. Encourage a discussion about the desire to fit in with peers and the feelings resulting from criticism about food and weight.

e. Allow time for completion; reinforce that poems or song lyrics need not rhyme, and that a limerick is a poetic form and lyrics are poems set to music.

f. Encourage teens to share their responses.

IV. Enrichment Activities
a. Group compositions
   - Ask teens to brainstorm limerick lines (or any type of poems) as a group.
   - A volunteer writes on the board as peers dictate the words.
   - They all read the finished product in unison.

b. Party Planning - Encourage teams or the whole group to develop party food menus that include healthy options and heartier fare (for those who want it). Examples:
   - Pizza with *the works*; but also offer veggie pizza.
   - Vegetable platter with low fat dip; a fruit tray; offer low-fat chocolate dip for decadent taste buds.
   - Make *do-it-yourself* sandwiches where teens can take more or less of meat, cheese, vegetables; have spreads such as mustard, ketchup, low-fat mayonnaise.

Food Fact Jeopardy

Category: Body Part Look-alikes

1. If you cut a carrot crosswise, what does it resemble and help, especially at night. *(Eye)*
2. What does a walnut with its two hemispheres resemble and help? *(Brain)*
3. What does celery look like and help? Humans have 206 of them. *(Bones)*
4. If you cut a tomato in half, what does it help and resemble with its chambers? *(Heart)*
5. What do grape branches and clusters resemble and help? They are in the lungs. *(Alveoli)*
6. If laid sideways, what sensory organ does a mushroom resemble and help? *(Ear)*
7. If this fruit is on your face with ends upward, it resembles a smile and helps mood. *(Banana)*

Category: Friendly Foods

1. Vitamin C foods are in what two colorful, crunchy food groups? *(Fruits and vegetables)*
2. What does tryptophan in poultry, fish, soy and other foods elevate? *(Mood)*
3. What vitamin complex helps the nervous system? *(Vitamin B)*
4. What vitamin helps bones and teeth? *(Vitamin D)*
5. What nutrient helps build muscle and is in meat, fish, eggs, soy and nuts? *(Protein)*
6. What substance, essential for life, helps chemical processes and removes toxins? *(Water)*
7. Small fish with edible bones like canned salmon are high in what mineral? *(Calcium)*

Category: Fact or Fiction?

1. Skipping meals helps you lose weight. *(Fiction; you get hungrier and may overeat.)*
2. You can eat starches like potatoes and pasta and lose weight. *(Fact; avoid fatty toppings and creamy sauces.)*
3. Brown eggs are more nutritious. *(Fiction; color indicates the hen's breed and feather color.)*
4. Fast food can be healthy. *(Fact; choose salads, grilled foods, fat free milk.)*
5. Grapefruit and cabbage burn fat. *(Fiction; no food burns fat. Exercise can raise metabolism.)*
6. Natural and herbal weight loss products are safe. *(Fiction; they are not tested for effectiveness or safety and some are dangerous.)*
7. Eating late at night is ok for weight loss. *(Fact; total daily intake and exercise matter, not time of day.)*

Category: Emotional or Physical Hunger?

1. You got good grades and craved pizza to celebrate. *(Emotional)*
2. You were stood up for a date and ate a half gallon of ice cream. *(Emotional)*
3. It has been five hours since your last meal and your stomach is rumbling. *(Physical)*
4. Your hunger came on suddenly and you want a certain food. *(Emotional)*
5. You stopped eating when you felt full and satisfied. *(Physical)*
6. You ate to feel better but felt worse and guilty. *(Emotional)*
7. You absent-mindedly ate the whole bag of chips. *(Emotional)*

TEENS – Body Image and Beyond

Food Fact Jeopardy

FOR THE FACILITATOR

I. Purpose

To recognize food's value, rather than just the taste or caloric content.

To differentiate fact from fiction and emotional from physical hunger.

II. General Comments

Teens educate themselves or reinforce familiar concepts by playing the game.

III. Possible Activities

a. If possible, (but not essential), display any or all of the following items, or use pictures:
   - Carrot
   - Walnut
   - Celery
   - Tomato
   - Grapes
   - Banana
   - Mushroom
   - Water

b. Ask for a volunteer who is comfortable reading aloud to be Game Show Host.

c. The remaining teens are contestants.

d. Give the *Food Fact Jeopardy* handout to the host who sits at the front of the room.

e. Remind host not to read the parenthesized answers aloud.

f. Teens take turns selecting a category. Write them on the board.
   - Body Part Look-alikes
   - Friendly Foods
   - Fact or Fiction?
   - Emotional or Physical Hunger?

g. The host reads a question, contestants answer; teens may ask peers for help if needed.

h. Emphasize that risk-taking and playing the game matter more than knowing an answer.

i. No one needs to be embarrassed for being unsure; peer help is available.

j. There are no points; no winners or losers. Teens play for fun and knowledge.

IV. Enrichment Activities

a. Write *Food: Friend or Foe?* on the board and encourage a discussion of its benefits and pleasures compared to the battles people have with eating too much or too little, and having the means to afford nutritious meals.

b. Ask teens if it is possible to have too much of a good thing.
   Elicit thoughtful points:
   - The correct vitamins, minerals, and other supplements and usage, need to be discussed with a physician before consumption. Some nutrients are dangerous if overtaken or if taken in combination with other nutrients or substances.
   - We are told to drink 6-8 glasses of water, but too little or too much water can be hazardous.

c. Ask teens to share their experiences and brainstorm ways to manage emotional hunger with pleasant diversions; to identify the emotion and the issues involved; to journal, talk, draw, write, enjoy music, or any other means of expression; to use coping skills like imagery, deep breathing, exercise, progressive muscle relaxation, meditation, spirituality or faith; to read inspirational literature; and to take on intellectual challenges like puzzles and brain games.

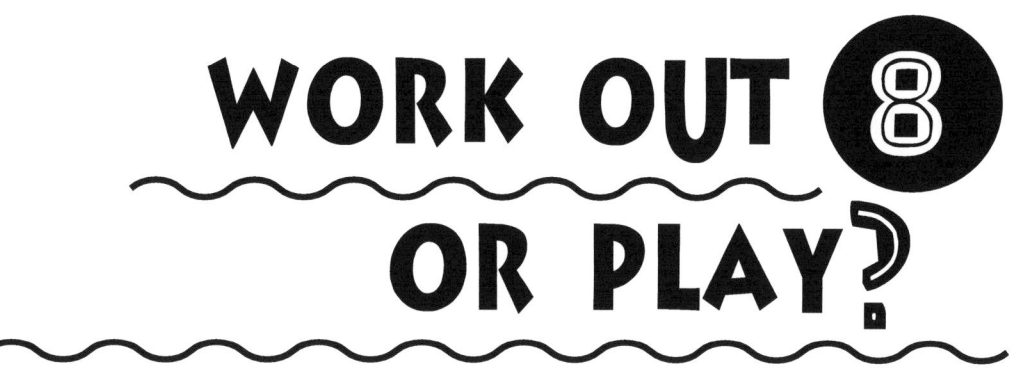
WORK OUT OR PLAY? 8

Do you know what my favorite part of the game is? The opportunity to play.
— MIKE SINGLETARY

Pics and Tips .... page 93 ▶
Through a Pictionary™ type game and charades, teens identify fitness activities and ways to improve sports skills.

A-Z Fitness .... page 95 ▶
Teams or individuals race to guess the fitness-related words and others.

Price Fair .... page 97 ▶
In a health fair or job fair format, teens circulate among stations sharing ideas for cost-cutting and fundraising for sports, lessons and related activities.

Work Out or Play?

Pics and Tips

Play Softball
Watch the ball to see if the pitch is a ball or strike, to decide whether to swing or not.

Play Soccer
Be ambidextrous. Whatever you can do with one foot you should be able to do with the other.

Play Basketball
Remember BEEFC: Balance, Eyes on the ball, Elbows in, Follow-through, Concentrate.

Play Volleyball
Less experienced players use underhand serves; more experienced players try overhand serves.

Play Badminton
Try to shoot backhand; it's harder for your opponent to hit these shots.

Play Tennis
When hitting, focus on fluidity, using both your upper and lower body.

Play Football
Play with bent knees. Straight knees and hips risk injuries.

Swim
Videotape your swimming technique. Review it with friends and receive suggestions.

Dance
Each type of dance requires specific shoes to protect legs and feet; be sure the size is right.

Walk
Walk fast enough to increase your pulse but be able to carry on a conversation; do not allow yourself to be out of breath.

Jog
Be sure your family and friends know when and where you'll be; avoid deserted and dark routes.

Do Aerobics
Listen to favorite tunes to motivate you during your work-out.

Ride a Bike
Select and set up your bike for your body size.

Lift Weights
Warm up first; lift and lower weights slowly; breathe, do not hold your breath.

Box
To block a solid punch, bend your knees, drop your hips and exhale.

Wrestle
Correct stance is body slightly forward, hands in front; move forward using the balls of your feet.

TEENS – Body Image and Beyond

Pics and Tips
FOR THE FACILITATOR

I. **Purpose**

   To consider many ways to exercise.

   To learn tips for improving skills in sports and fitness activities.

II. **General Comments**

   This session provides a guessing game to be played by drawing pictures on the board, or by using body language as in Charades.

III. **Possible Activities**

   a. Before session, photocopy the *Pics and Tips* handout and cut on the broken lines.
   b. Fold the strips of paper and place them in a cup or container.
   c. If available, a sports cap, baseball glove or boxing glove is an interesting container.
   d. Tell teens they will be guessing sports and fitness activities, and ways to improve their performance.
   e. Tell them when it is their turn they will do the following:
      - Pick up a slip of paper out of the container.
      - Draw on the board, or portray with pantomime, the sport or activity, as peers try to guess it.
      - Then, the same teen draws or demonstrates the accompanying performance pointer.
      - Teens are not expected to guess every word verbatim; just the gist of the pointer.
      - The first teen to guess the performance pointer correctly, takes the next turn by pulling a new slip of paper.

IV. **Enrichment Activities**

   a. Encourage teens to share their experiences with different types of exercise or sports and to brainstorm performance pointers.
   b. Encourage a discussion of other activities specific to their geographic region such as ice skating, skiing, mountain climbing, rock climbing, rowing, snorkeling, etc.
   c. Encourage teens with similar interests to sit in clusters to discuss their sport; then the whole group reconvenes; a spokesperson for each cluster shares what they discussed.
   d. Encourage teens to plan dream vacations and include locations conducive to their favorite activities.
   e. Encourage brainstorming ways to get into an activity or sport and how to access low cost lessons and gear.

Work Out or Play?

A-Z Fitness

For each letter, guess the activity or sports-related word, based on the hint.
Then add an activity or sports-related word that starts with the same letter. See (A) example.

Letter	Hint	Guess the word related to fitness	Add another word related to fitness
(A)	*Example: Bow and arrows are used.*	archery	aerobics
B	Done in a ring		
C	Person who stands behind home plate		
D	Gainer, swan, back-flip, tuck		
E	Objects used in sports or for safety		
F	Fighting with swords		
G	Place: games, work-outs, Phys. Ed.		
H	Done on trails		
I	Exercising early in the day helps		
J	Running at a slow steady pace		
K	Down for the count		
L	Often injured; tissue connecting bones		
M	Long distance running event		
N	Provides fuel; needed for health & life		
O	Healthy exercise and nutrition helps		
P	Small disk of hard rubber		
Q	Case to carry or hold arrows		
R	Similar to football, started in the U.K.		
S	Done on snowy slopes, or flat land		
T	Singles and doubles matches		
U	Pitch: hand brought forward and up		
V	Played on floors, with net		
W	Team water sport involving a ball		
X	Diagnostic tool for sports injuries		Bonus point
Y	Set of postures & breathing exercises		
Z	Brazilian dance and aerobics		

© 2013 WHOLE PERSON ASSOCIATES, 101 WEST 2ND ST., SUITE 203, DULUTH MN 55802 • 800-247-6789

TEENS – Body Image and Beyond

A-Z Fitness

FOR THE FACILITATOR

I. Purpose
To consider exercise and sports options and some related terms.

To have fun with a team or individual race to finish the activity.

II. General Comments
Teens need to have fun exercising and to enjoy an activity that makes them think of options.

III. Possible Activities
a. Before session, decide if teams or individuals will *race*.
b. Write the word *Fitness* on the board and discuss the many ways one can become fit.
c. Tell teens they will be racing by guessing and adding fitness words.
d. Divide the teens into teams; team members sit in clusters out of hearing range of others. If the activity is to be done individually, no special seating arrangements are required.
e. Explain that no one is allowed to touch a pen or pencil until the contest starts.
f. Distribute the *A-Z Fitness* handout, review the instructions and example.
g. After you say Go! whichever team or individual finishes first (with logical responses) wins.
h. If no one finishes by ten minutes before group time ends, whoever has the most words wins.
i. Review *Guess* words; then ask teens to share their *Add another word related to fitness* words for letters of alphabet.

Answers below for *Guess the word related to fitness* column and *Add another word related to fitness* column; (for *Add another word related to fitness*, accept any logical words for each letter of the alphabet).

(A see example) B boxing baseball	G gymnasium gymnastics	L ligament league	Q quiver quarterback	V volleyball victory
C catcher cheerleader	H hiking horseback	M marathon martial arts	R rugby roller skate	W water polo wrestling
D diving dancing	I insomnia ice-skating	N nutrient net	S skiing soccer	X x-ray bonus point given
E equipment energy	J jogging jump rope	O obesity oar	T tennis t-ball	Y yoga yard-line
F fencing football	K knockout kick boxing	P puck paddleball	U underhand umpire	Z zumba zeal

IV. Enrichment Activities
- Ask teens to share types of sports and exercise they like and dislike and why.
- Ask teens to bring in or share a photograph of something they have done for fun. It's fun to be fit!

Work Out or Play?

Price Fair

Ways to save money on equipment, clothing and involvement:

1.
2.
3.
4.
5.
6.
7.
8.
9.
10.

Places to find reasonably priced activities:

1.
2.
3.
4.
5.
6.
7.
8.
9.
10.

Ways for individuals to earn money:

1.
2.
3.
4.
5.
6.
7.
8.
9.
10.

Team fundraising ideas:

1.
2.
3.
4.
5.
6.
7.
8.
9.
10.

TEENS – Body Image and Beyond

Price Fair

FOR THE FACILITATOR

I. Purpose
To determine economical ways to participate in sports and exercise in a job fair or health fair format.

II. General Comments
Many teens are excluded from sports as school athletic funding is cut; students must pay to play in some school districts. Parents say *No* or struggle to afford fees, lessons, clothes, shoes, equipment, gas and travel.

III. Possible Activities
a. Before session, cut the reproducible page into four sections as indicated by broken lines.
b. Volunteer writers will each take one section and station themselves around the room.
c. Teens will walk to each station and give their opinions to the volunteer writers.
d. Alternately, four large sheets of sticky chart paper are labeled and placed on walls.
e. Labels will correspond to the headings on the handout, *Price Fair*.
f. Encourage a brief discussion about the expenses involved in playing sports, and taking lessons.
g. Tell teens they will visit four stations, like at a job fair or health fair, and give their ideas to the volunteer recorders or write on chart paper; topics involve money issues for sports and activities.
h. Volunteers write peers' ideas on the cut-out list or encourage teens to write on the chart paper.
i. After teens speak or write their ideas at each station they return to their seats.
j. Each volunteer shares the ideas recorded on paper or reads what peers wrote on the chart paper.

IV. Enrichment Activities – Possible ideas::

a. Ways to save money on equipment, clothing and involvement:
1. Buy used merchandise
2. Exchange no longer needed items
3. Buy at end of season or off season sales
4. Buy interchangeable items for various sports
5. Register for classes or teams early
6. Choose less expensive sports
7. Think twice about costly sports
8. Walking or jogging is free
9. Aerobics or dance CD is a one time cost
10. Take your own team photos

b. Places to find reasonably priced activities:
1. Join recreation leagues or school teams
2. YWCA and YMCA
3. Boys and Girls Clubs of America
4. City pools
5. State Parks
6. Local Departments of Parks and Recreation
7. Local Community Centers
8. School pools and gyms
9. Community colleges
10. Community or religious youth groups

c. Ways to earn money individually:
1. Sell items you no longer need
2. Recruit friends for a garage or yard sale
3. Walk and take care of others' pets
4. Tutor in a subject in which you excel
5. Teach what you know
6. Help people with computers and electronics
7. Provide a service: shovel snow, mow lawns
8. Babysit, deliver newspapers or work
9. Combine work with your sports passion
10. Collect and redeem recyclable cans, etc.

d. Team fundraising ideas:
1. Car wash
2. Auction donated merchandise
3. Bake sale
4. Host a dance, music, or barbeque event
5. Host a face painting event for local kids
6. Sell items, i.e., grapefruit
7. Check out online fundraising ideas
8. Wash outside windows at others' homes
9. Host a pet show or talent show
10. Host poetry, art or other contest

SEXUAL IMAGE

Love makes your soul crawl out from it's hiding place.
— Zora Neale Hurston

Transbodies .... page 101 ▶
Teens consider whether gender identity issues are affecting their body image; they are directed to professionals with expertise regarding related emotional, physical and interpersonal issues.

Puppet? Marionette? Your Own Person?   page 103 ▶
Teens decide whether they are self-directed, or dancing on a string to please a dating partner regarding appearance.

MAGNETISM .... page 105 ▶
Teens identify endearing and enduring traits that are more magnetic than superficial sex-appeal.

Sexual Image ▶

Transbodies

Sexual identity relates to male or female gender, both outside and inside. Transgender people think, feel, act, or look different from the body they were born with. Females may hate their breasts; males may hate their muscles, facial and body hair. They may cross-dress or seek a sexual reassignment surgery. They feel trapped in a body that disguises who they really are.

Who are you inside? Use symbols or drawings to show you as your chosen gender, whether or not it matches your outer body. Show this with body build, facial or no facial hair, etc.; avoid drawing private parts.

In the illustration above, depict around you, like a collage, what you would be doing, and ways your life might be different emotionally and socially, if you were your chosen gender.

Or...

If you are comfortable that your inner gender matches your outer body, depict ways your life might be better if there were no gender related stereotypes or sexual discrimination. Maybe you would choose a sport, career, dance class, hobby or other activity not usually associated with your gender.

List the first three steps you think people who are dissatisfied with their gender should take.

a. _____

b. _____

c. _____

TEENS – Body Image and Beyond

Transbodies

FOR THE FACILITATOR

I. Purpose
To recognize whether gender identity issues are adversely affecting body image.

To seek counseling and medical advice regarding options.

To acknowledge a discrepancy (if it exists) between inner and outer gender traits.

II. General Comments
Teens, especially at puberty, may have sexual identity issues and may wish they were the opposite sex. For some this may be a stage that passes; for others it is a culmination of what they (and possibly their parents) have long suspected. Teens who dress or act like the opposite sex are at great risk for being victims of bullying or violence; they often are depressed and may resort to self-harm and suicide. Modern medicine can suspend puberty with hormone blockers to give the teen, family, therapist, physician, etc. time to determine the best course of action. Controversy exists regarding whether and when to start cross sex medicines to enable the teen to develop the preferred secondary sexual characteristics, (facial and body hair for aspiring males; breasts and less hair for aspiring females, etc.). Sexual reassignment surgery is generally not allowed until age 18.

III. Possible Activities
a. Write *congruence* and *incongruence* on the board and ask their definitions. Elicit that congruence means similarity; incongruence means not similar; ideally there is congruence between our inner and outer selves.

b. Encourage a discussion of ways people are one way on the outside but actually, much different inside. Examples:
   - Putting on a happy face but being depressed
   - Acting confident but feeling afraid
   - Being thin but feeling overweight.

c. Explain that today's session addresses an issue some might be uncomfortable about and that jokes or snickers may be tempting, but the subject is serious.

d. Emphasize that teens attempted or died by suicide related to the issue, particularly if bullied.

e. Remind teens their responses are private; sharing is strictly voluntary.

f. Distribute the *Transbodies* handout and allow time for completion.

g. Encourage a discussion of steps a potentially transgender teen might take:
   - Tell parents or a trusted family member.
   - Find a therapist experienced with this issue.
   - See a physician and a specialist who deals with transgender treatments.
   - See a psychiatrist in case depression or other conditions require medications.
   - Seek spiritual counsel.

h. Encourage disclosures of their responses or drawings within their comfort zones.

IV. Enrichment Activities
a. Encourage brainstorming (while a volunteer lists their ideas on the board) regarding the pros and cons of puberty blocking and cross sex hormones being prescribed for teens.

b. Encourage teens to share their opinions regarding what is the appropriate age for sexual reassignment surgery and reasons.

Sexual Image

Puppet? Marionette? Your Own Person?

1. Who or what controls a hand puppet?

2. Who or what controls a marionette?

3. Who or what controls you by telling you what your face or body should look like?

4. In what ways is someone telling you what to say and how to change your behavior?

5. In what ways are you dancing on a string to please others by your appearance?

6. Who or what controls the independent person?

7. What does a light bulb represent, or a light bulb moment?

8. In what ways does your light bulb affect how you look and act?

9. Would you rather be a puppet, a marionette or your own person and why?

TEENS – Body Image and Beyond

Puppet? Marionette? Your Own Person?

FOR THE FACILITATOR

I. Purpose
To become more self-directed regarding face and figure, versus excess exercising, dieting, altering appearance or behavior to appeal to dating partners and/or standards of a clique.

II. General Comments
Teens often let the image-crazed media or peers dictate how they should look and act. They need encouragement to be driven by their own motives, versus unknowingly being manipulated.

III. Possible Activities
a. If possible show a puppet, marionette, or light bulb; ask teens to be thinking about these objects.

b. Write Ventriloquist on the board and ask its meaning. *(A person who changes his or her voice so it seems to be coming from a puppet.)*

c. Encourage teens to share times when someone tried to speak for them or overly control their movements.

d. Distribute the *Puppet? Marionette? Your Own Person?* handout and allow time for completion.

e. Encourage teens to share their responses.

f. Encourage a discussion of the disadvantages of puppet-hood and advantages of self-direction.

IV. Enrichment Activities
a. Light Bulb Moments: Encourage teens to share their light bulb moments, times of sudden hindsight, foresight and insight; discuss that self-directed people light their own way and do not hide their own light or identity.

b. Scenarios: The facilitator reads aloud the situations below and teens describe what they would do; teens then state whether they would resemble a puppet, a marionette or an independent person.

c. Situations to be read aloud are bulleted; do not reveal the possible responses unless teens cannot come up with their own ideas.

- Your dating partner broke up with you because of another person's looks. Since the break-up you feel isolated and unattractive, like no one will ever care for you again. What would you do?
Possible responses: A puppet might lie crumbled in a heap or dance on the string of extreme measures to look better; a person might join a club and seek people with common interests instead of meeting partners obsessed with looks.

- You are attracted to a fitness enthusiast but you dislike exercise. What would you do?
Possible responses: A puppet might over-zealously pursue a disliked sport, seeking approval; a person might decide to warm the bench at the fitness fanatic's events.

- You hardly ever date. Your friends say if you want dates you need to gain or lose weight, color your hair or get a surgical procedure. What would you do?
Possible responses: A puppet might make all the changes to please people; a person might evaluate the suggestions but make an independent decision about how to deal with the situation.

d. Encourage a discussion with this prompt: *Is it possible to be too much of your own person?* Elicit that being an independent person entails open-minded receptivity to suggestions and ideas, but self-directed decisions.

Sexual Image

MAGNETISM

What does a magnet do? _____

What kind of people do you want in your magnetic field?

    a. _____

    b. _____

    c. _____

Around the magnet write five of your non-physical pulling power traits.

List five values you want your relationships based on:

    1. _____

    2. _____

    3. _____

    4. _____

    5. _____

State whether you think looks or personality have more staying power and explain why.

_____

_____

_____

TEENS – Body Image and Beyond

MAGNETISM

FOR THE FACILITATOR

I. Purpose
To consider elements of selfhood and relationships beyond physical attraction.

II. General Comments
Obviously, teens want to attract dating partners; many starve, binge, purge, eat excessively, say yes when wanting to say no, or obsess about their looks for the sake of romance.

III. Possible Activities
  a. If possible, show a magnet and tell teens they will be thinking about magnetic attraction.
  b. Write *Sex appeal* on the board and ask teens what it means.
  c. Notice their responses and comment on whether they are primarily physically focused, or that they are considering aspects like confidence or caring about people.
  d. Distribute the *Magnetism* handout and allow time for completion.
  e. Encourage teens to share their responses.

IV. Enrichment Activities
  a. Encourage a discussion with the prompt *Do Opposites Attract? Why or Why Not?*
  b. Discuss that partners may have similar values such as honesty and generosity but be opposites in other ways: extrovert and introvert; one might be a math whiz and the other artistic, etc.
  c. Ask teens to brainstorm personality traits they dislike; a volunteer writes their ideas on the board.

  Examples to elicit:
  - Dishonesty
  - Disrespect
  - Drinking
  - Scary risk-taking

  d. Encourage a discussion regarding the power of a positive or negative attitude to draw out the best or worst in themselves and their dating partners.

  Examples to elicit:
  - If they feel worthy of love, it is likely they will have a healthy relationship.
  - If they are obsessed with fear of infidelity, constant accusations may push a partner away.

BEYOND BODY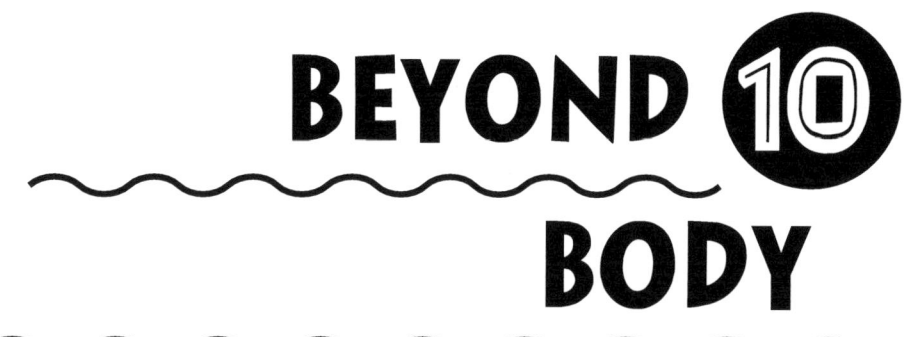

To be a hero or heroine, one must give an order to oneself.
— SIMONE WEIL

Body Idioms Art and Reflections .... page 109 ▶
Teens draw or write to reveal issues and discover creative solutions.

Charades .... page 111 ▶
Through playing charades, teens apply figurative bodily expressions to current or recent situations and emotions.

Blinders: On or Off? .... page 113 ▶
On a race diagram, teens depict or describe distractions and negativity to block out and describe how to reach the finish line; conversely, teens note when to remove blinders for a better perspective.

What's Eating You? .... page 115 ▶
Teens label sharks with issues and emotions that consume them; teens match devourers with their positive replacements.

Character-Clues .... page 117 ▶
Teens play a word game that prioritizes character building over body-building or beauty; they describe ways to exemplify internal attributes.

Pro and Con .... page 119 ▶
Teens determine how they would handle ethical dilemmas; then individually or by playing a game, teens weigh pros and cons of possible actions.

Self-Centered or Not in Vain? .... page 123 ▶
If I Can Stop One Heart from Breaking *by Emily Dickenson helps teens make their lives count.*

Never Say Never .... page 125 ▶
Compensation *by E.M. Brainard describes how adversity is part of achievement; teens personalize the concepts.*

SILENT HEROES .... page 127 ▶
In honor of the Sandy Hook Elementary School shooting victims, teens pledge and plan random acts of kindness; teens consider the Levels of Charity *written by Maimonides in the 12th century.*

Beyond Body

Body Idioms Art and Reflections

Head in the Clouds
My head is in the clouds but my feet are on the ground and my heart is in the right place.
What is your head dreaming? What are you doing? What are your motives?

Nose out of Joint
My nose is out of joint; it is written all over my face; and I'm up to my eyeballs.
What upset you? What are you feeling? What is overwhelming or suffocating you?

Hard to Swallow
It's hard to swallow; I have a gut feeling, and I am washing my hands of it.
What is hard to accept? What do you know in your gut? What are you getting rid of and how?

Hands are Tied
My hands are tied but I'll rack my brain, use elbow grease, and dig in my heels.
How will you use brain power, hard work and determination to surmount what seems to hinder you?

Let my Hair Down
I'll let my hair down, get my problems off of my chest and take a weight off my shoulders.
What do you need to be real about? What do you need to express? How will this lighten your load?

Achilles' Heel
I had an eye opener and came to my senses about my Achilles' heel.
What did you see, hear, and realize? What is your Achilles' heel (weakness, downfall, vulnerability)?

Warts and All
Take me warts and all, with egg on my face. I am more than meets the eye.
Show or describe your identity that is above and beyond faults and embarrassments.

Vented my Spleen
I vented my spleen; now they're up in arms. We need a heart to heart talk.
How did you spill your guts? Who is angry? What needs to be understood?

TEENS – Body Image and Beyond

Body Idioms Art and Reflections
FOR THE FACILITATOR

I. Purpose
To use figurative bodily expressions to elicit thoughts and feelings, visually and/or verbally.

II. General Comments
Drawing or using symbols helps many teens uncover issues and discover creative solutions. Alternately, teens may relate to the idioms verbally.

III. Possible Activities
  a. Decide before session whether teens will self-select their activity or whether you will assign the same one, or different ones, to everyone; either way, there are eight options for eight sessions.
  b. Write *Pain in the neck* on the board, and ask its meaning; explain *an idiom is an expression whose meaning is not the same as the individual words, such as, "walk on eggs" which means walk or talk very carefully.*
  c. Tell teens they will draw and/or write about themselves related to common expressions.
  d. Remind teens that artistic talent, perfect spelling or grammar are not required; the goal is to show thoughts and feelings with pictures, symbols, or words to bring out inner wisdom.
  e. If using one topic for everyone, write it on the board; if you are giving different topics to teens, cut topics out and distribute; otherwise distribute the *Body Idioms Art or Reflections* handout and let teens choose one of the eight to draw and/or write about.
  f. Allow time for completion.
  g. Encourage teens to share their work within their level of comfort; do not force disclosure.

IV. Enrichment Activities
Encourage teens to brainstorm other idioms, and apply them to their lives. Possibilities:
  - Keep your nose clean.
  - Have nerves of steel.
  - Keep your head above water.
  - Knock you over with a feather.
  - Keep your nose to the grindstone.
  - Have the gift of gab.
  - If push comes to shove …
  - Music to your ears …
  - Be on your last legs.
  - Be wet behind the ears.
  - A sight for sore eyes…
  - Play it by ear.

Charades

We're going to play charades. Familiarize yourself with these expressions.

I am in water over my head when …

I wear my heart on my sleeve regarding …

My heart goes out to …

I lend a hand when …

My head is spinning about …

I have the upper hand when …

I pay through the nose for …

I pull someone's leg when …

I stick out like a sore thumb when …

I shoot myself in the foot when …

I jump out of my skin when …

I'm able to breathe easily when …

I keep my ear to the ground about …

I am really in hot water when …

I bite my tongue about …

I put my foot in my mouth when …

I cannot stomach …

My back is against the wall regarding …

I have butterflies in my stomach when …

What's being forced down my throat is …

I give blood, sweat and tears for …

TEENS – Body Image and Beyond

Charades

FOR THE FACILITATOR

I. **Purpose**
   To apply figurative bodily expressions to current or recent issues.

II. **General Comments**
   Charades are fun, require creativity and draw teens out of their comfort zones as they portray humorous and serious idioms.

III. **Possible Activities**
   a. Ask teens about their experiences playing Charades.
   b. Distribute the *Charades* handout.
   c. Ask the group if they know them meaning of *idiom*. If not, explain, an idiom is an expression whose meaning is not the same as the individual words such as *I walk on eggs*, which means walk or talk very carefully.
   d. Decide whether to have teens complete the sentences in writing first or to play Charades immediately.
   e. If they write completions, they turn over their papers afterward; alternately they read the list to familiarize themselves with the idioms and then turn over their papers.
   f. The audience must not look at the list after the initial exposure noted above.
   g. Only the teen taking a turn portraying an idiom may refer to the list.
   h. Charades rules:
      - A volunteer takes his/her paper to the front of the room and wordlessly, using body language, portrays an idiom.
      - Peers take turns guessing without peeking at their papers.
      - The teen who guesses correctly applies the expression to his/her life, then takes a turn portraying an idiom.
      - If teens who already portrayed idioms guess correctly, peers who have not yet played are given a chance.

IV. **Enrichment Activities**
   a. If not already done, ask teens to complete the sentences in writing, then share their responses.
   b. Ask teens to brainstorm idioms they have heard or to make up their own.
   c. It is helpful to think of body parts, then recall related idioms and apply them to personal experiences.
      Examples:
      - Head: Keep my head on straight, lose my head, …
      - Teeth: Give my eye teeth; by the skin of my teeth, …
      - Neck: Neck and neck; breathing down my neck, …
      - Throat: Have a lump in my throat; go for the jugular, …
      - Shoulder: Get the cold shoulder; chip on my shoulder, …
      - Arm: Arm myself; give an arm and a leg, …
      - Back: Behind my back; be stabbed in my back; back-bite, …
      - Chest: Not holding my breath; take my breath away, …
      - Skin: Get goose bumps; feel my flesh crawl, be thin or thick skinned, …
      - Bones: Skeleton in my closet; bone chilling, …

Beyond Body

Blinders: On or Off?

Imagine yourself to be this teen with blinders running on a race track toward the finish line. Draw on the illustration and/or write to respond to the questions below.

My finish line for this race is… _____

_____

My most helpful lesson learned… _____

_____

Distractions to block out … _____

_____

Negativity to ignore … _____

_____

What I need to do now… _____

_____

I need to see the whole picture regarding … _____

_____

TEENS – Body Image and Beyond

Blinders: On or Off?

FOR THE FACILITATOR

I. Purpose
To consider that horses run their own races by blocking out distractions and focusing on the goal.

To keep in mind lessons learned from the past; to do first things first on the way to the finish line.

II. General Comments
Describing or depicting the next step and planning action-oriented goals helps teens achieve. Teens focus on their personal best and ignore potential competitors. Teens also consider when to remove blinders that block options or truths.

III. Possible Activities
a. Before session, enlist a volunteer, who will walk into the room with blinders, (paper held at sides of head to block peripheral vision).
b. Ask teens when blinders are used and why, (horse races; horses run straighter and faster).
c. Explain that figurative blinders can help teens focus on their goals
d. Distribute *Blinders On or Off?* and allow time for completion.
e. Teens may use words, drawings, symbols or caricatures to describe or depict their ideas.
f. Encourage teens to share their responses.
g. Discuss how blinders prevent horses from seeing who is closing in from behind or running neck and neck with them; encourage teens to run their own races and downplay what perceived competitors are doing.
h. Encourage a discussion about what to do before putting on blinders and focusing on a path.
   Possibilities:
   - Look around to determine what goals and paths are available; decide which race to run.
   - Look for ways to carve a new path if needed.
   - Identify people and external sources of help or advice.
   - Look within for endurance and spiritual strength.

IV. Enrichment Activities
a. Ask teens to brainstorm times when blinders need to be taken off, to expose themselves to realities they have denied.
b. A volunteer lists their ideas.
   Possibilities:
   - Seeing both positive and negative traits in dating partners and friends.
   - Acknowledging and learning form mistakes.
   - Admitting issues that need to be addressed and asking for help.
   - Being open-minded to adult advice and concerns; seeing the other person's point of view.
c. Write this George Sheehan quote on the board; ask teens to apply it to their lives:

> ***It's very hard in the beginning to understand that the whole idea is not to beat the other runners. Eventually you will learn that the competition is against the little voice inside you that wants you to quit.***

d. Write this Steve Prefontaine quote on the board; ask teens to apply it to their lives:

> ***Most people run a race to see who is fastest.***
> ***I run a race to see who has the most guts.***

Beyond Body

What's Eating You?

Feelings and problems can consume you; they eat away at your peace, joy, aspirations and positive aspects of you and your life.

In the picture below, label the three sharks (devourers) with emotions or issues that are trying to destroy you.

What are they taking from you? _____

_____

_____

Match the numbers of the devourers with the letters of their positive replacements.

DEVOURERS
1. Anger and resentment
2. Guilt and shame
3. Fear and anxiety
4. Sadness and self-pity
5. Loneliness
6. Inferiority
7. Envy and jealousy
8. Grief and loss
9. Being abused
10. Alcohol and drugs
11. Greed and selfishness
12. Laziness or low motivation

POSITIVE REPLACEMENTS
A. Make a gratitude list.
B. Forgive, for your own sake.
C. Tell a trusted adult.
D. Focus on positive attributes.
E. Do what you are afraid to do, if it is safe.
F. Forgive yourself; make amends if possible.
G. Help others (tutor, feed the homeless, walk shelter animals).
H. Find your passion.
I. Give something to someone or use your gifts to benefit others.
J. Keep happy memories alive.
K. Value your uniqueness; don't compare self with others, (apples and oranges).
L. Seek help from professionals and people who have been there, done that.

TEENS – Body Image and Beyond

What's Eating You?

FOR THE FACILITATOR

I. Purpose
To identify feelings and issues that can overwhelm teens and reflect on positive replacements.

II. General Comments
Teens need help to identify destructive elements in their lives. They may divert their attention from real emotions and issues by obsessing about body image. Teens are encouraged to look at what bothers them and what might benefit them.

III. Possible Activities
a. Ask teens to describe what happens in computer games like Pac-Man.
b. Ask teens to share thoughts about horror movies or nature documentaries where creatures eat prey.
c. Distribute the *What's Eating You* handout and allow time for completion.
d. Encourage teens to share their responses.
e. Allow any responses that teens can substantiate. Possible responses are:
   1. B
   2. F
   3. E
   4. A
   5. G
   6. D
   7. K
   8. J
   9. C
   10. L
   11. I
   12. H
f. Ask teens to share positive replacements that have helped them in addition to those in the matching exercise

IV. Enrichment Activities
a. Ask teens to share their *devourers*, which may be different from those listed in the matching exercise.
   Possibilities:
   - Time wasters like excessive time on social networks or addiction to video games.
   - Negative self-talk or destructive criticism from significant others.
b. Ask peers to brainstorm positive replacements while a volunteer lists them on paper to give to each teen who shares.
   Possibilities for the examples above:
   - Set a schedule for study, exercise and other activities and stick to it.
   - Use positive self-talk and be assertive with demoralizing people.

Beyond Body

Character-Clues

Above each set of boxes are character-clues. Fill in the boxes with the correct letters.
Choose from the *word bank* below.

| justice competence altruism conviction respect character humility connection responsibility compassion assertiveness joyfulness confidence restraint cooperation aspirations honesty |

C WORDS

Ability and know-how

Belief, trust

Bonds with people and organizations

Consideration, caring, empathy

Self-worth, self-reliance

Sense of right and wrong, morality, integrity

Teamwork, collaboration

R WORDS

Regard for others

Reliability, trustworthiness

Self-control, self-discipline

H WORDS

Truthfulness, openness

Unassuming, meek

A WORDS

Boldness, strong in stating a position

Hopes, ambitions, goals

Selfless, benefitting others

J WORDS

Cheerfulness, happiness

Fairness, impartiality

TEENS – Body Image and Beyond

Character-Clues
FOR THE FACILITATOR

I. Purpose
To encourage teens to recognize and develop positive traits.

II. General Comments
Teens need to focus on character building, versus over-emphasis on body building and external beauty. Teens play a team game and then share how they, or someone they know, exemplify the attributes.

III. Possible Activities
1. **Team Game:**
   a. Before session copy the *word bank* from the *Character Clues* handout onto the board.
   b. Provide a volunteer game show host with the *Character Clues* handout.
   c. Divide the group into two teams; members sit near each other to collaborate.
   d. Teams take turns selecting a category:
      (C WORDS, R WORDS, H WORDS, A WORDS OR J WORDS).
   e. Host copies one of the word boxes on the board and reads its clue or definition aloud.
   f. Teammates guess the correct word from the *word bank* on the board.
   g. If the first team misses, the second team tries.
   h. Teams try alternately until one team guesses correctly; host then writes the letters in the boxes.
   i. Erase each word box as it is completed but leave the *word bank* on the board.
   j. The first turn for the next word goes to the team that lost the previous round.
   k. A volunteer scorekeeper keeps track of which team correctly guesses each word.
   l. The team who correctly guesses the most words wins.
   m. The answers for the game show host are in this order:
      - C = competence, conviction, connection, compassion, confidence, character, cooperation
      - R = respect, responsibility, restraint
      - H = honesty, humility
      - A = assertiveness, aspirations, altruism
      - J = joyfulness, justice

2. **Individual Activity**
   Individual teens or teams write their responses on the handout and then share with the group.

IV. Enrichment Activities
   a. Ask teens to take turns sharing how they personally, or someone they know, exemplifies each of the words in the game.
   b. Give teens scenarios and ask them to guess the trait portrayed. Examples:
      - You see a peer sitting alone at lunch and invite the person to join you. (compassion)
      - You feel angry and ready to swear but count to ten or walk away. (restraint)
      - You can see a smart student's answers on a test, but do not cheat. (character, honesty)
      - You tutor students in a subject you know well. (altruism)
      - You ask for and accept help or tutoring in a subject that is difficult for you. (humility)
      - You say *no* to dangerous options; you express opinions firmly. (assertiveness)
      - You are judging a contest; you pick the best performer, not your best friend. (justice)
      - You have and hold hopes and dreams despite other people putting them down. (aspirations)
      - You seek people with similar values and belong to clubs, religious or spiritual groups, etc. (connection)

Beyond Body

Pro and Con

Dating

1. Your best friend's partner asks you out.
   a. You say *Yes* because you have been wanting to go out with the partner.
   b. You say *No, not until you break up with my friend.*
   c. You say *No* and tell your friend the partner cheats, (not revealing you were asked out).
   d. You say *No* and tell your friend that you were approached by the partner.

2. Your partner pressures you to have sex.
   a. You tell yourself, *it will keep my partner dating me.*
   b. You say you will only if it is safe sex.
   c. You say *No*, you are saving that for a future committed relationship or marriage.
   d. You say you'll think about it.

3. Your partner asks to drive your parents' car but you promised only you would drive.
   a. You let your partner drive because you want to keep the relationship going.
   b. You tell your partner, *Maybe next time.*
   c. You tell your partner the truth saying, *I promised my parents.*
   d. You decide to leave the car home and take the bus; avoid the issue entirely.

Friends

4. Your opinions on subjects like abortion and gay marriage differ from your friends' views. When they discuss these issues,
   a. You keep quiet or say you are undecided.
   b. You tell them they are wrong and substantiate your opinions.
   c. You tell them your opinion differs and why.
   d. You find new friends who agree with you.

5. Two of your friends are gossiping about a third friend. You know juicy tidbits to add fuel to the flame.
   a. You tell all; they have a right to know, and they'll like that you are giving them info.
   b. You say nothing and don't want to damage your friend's reputation.
   c. You tell your friend what the others say behind his/her back.
   d. You stick up for the friend who is being gossiped about.

6. Your best buddy wants you to try out for his team but you fear failure. You …
   a. Give it your best shot.
   b. Make an excuse and avoid the challenge.
   c. Say *Yes*; then you limp and say you hurt your ankle on the day of the try-outs.
   d. Share your fears and ask for pointers on performing your best.

(continued on the next page)

Pro and Con *(continued)*

School

7. Your friend has confiscated a copy of tomorrow's exam and invites you to collaborate on answers.
   a. You do it. You justify it by saying, *it's just this one time.*
   b. You say, *No, thank you*, and do nothing else.
   c. You say, *No*, and anonymously report your friend to the principal.
   d. You tell your friend that it's wrong.
8. You are being bullied.
   a. You anonymously tell a trusted friend, family member, teacher or counselor.
   b. Ignore the person(s).
   c. Take it to heart, feel devastated, overeat, drink, drug, and/or drop out of school.
   d. Decide you will get revenge.
9. You earned poor grades.
   a. You ask teachers what free help is available; you ask your parents to pay for tutoring.
   b. You decide you are hopeless and give up; drop out at the earliest age possible.
   c. You figure out what you are best at and pursue those studies.
   d. You figure out what is causing your declined performance and how you can rectify it.
10. Your parents insist on your going to a university; you love auto mechanics/cosmetology and want to go to a vocational school because of your interests.
    a. You please your parents; try a community college for a year, with an open mind.
    b. You stick to your career goals and apply for technical training.
    c. You take aptitude, interest, and career assessment inventories and share the results with your parents.
    d. You ask a teacher or counselor to talk to your parents in your presence.

Work

1. You are running a yard sale for your team or organization and a woman gives you two twenties stuck together for a twenty dollar item.
   a. Give her back the extra twenty dollar bill.
   b. Keep it; you justify it because you really need it.
   c. Turn it in to the cash box for the team or organization.
   d. Give her a ten dollar bill back, (say it was stuck to her twenty); keep five and turn in five to the organization.
2. You are tired from a late date last night.
   a. You call in sick.
   b. You go to work and do your best.
   c. You go to work but ask to leave early.
   d. You call and say you will be two hours late.
3. You know a co-worker is stealing from the company.
   a. Report the person to the supervisor.
   b. Mind your own business; keep quiet.
   c. Tell the co-worker to stop; threaten to tell the boss if the stealing continues.
   d. Encourage the co-worker to repay the money or admit the truth to the employer.
4. You are offered a promotion at work but it requires more hours which interferes with study time and sports. You …
   a. Turn it down due to other priorities.
   b. Accept it; better pay and prestige supersede grades and sports.
   c. Discuss the opportunity with family and friends.
   d. Try to negotiate a compromise about the number of extra hours required.

(continued on the next page)

Beyond Body

Pro and Con (continued)

Altruism

5. You overhear a cleaning person telling co-workers about a painful back but how badly the job is needed. You walk into the lavatory and see tons of paper towels all over the floor.
   a. You ignore it; it's not your problem.
   b. You tell another cleaning person about it who might pick them up.
   c. You pick them up, put them into trash; wash your hands.
   d. You tell the vice-principal that students are being sloppy in the bathroom.

6. Your parents can no longer pay for the lawn crew.
   a. You offer to do it for nothing.
   b. You offer to do it for half price.
   c. You convince your parents that if you spend time on the yard, your grades will suffer.
   d. You say you will do it for free once weekly if they lend you the car once weekly.

7. An elderly neighbor says he is ill and needs some things at the drugstore.
   a. You suggest he find a pharmacy that delivers.
   b. You offer to pick up the items for a small fee and gas money.
   c. You just pick up the items.
   d. You arrange for yourself and some trustworthy friends to volunteer to shop for shut-ins.

Problems

8. You smell alcohol on the breath of someone in your youth group. You are a recovering alcoholic, sober six months, but nobody in the group knows it.
   a. You ignore the problem; it's none of your business.
   b. You anonymously tell the group leader who will know what to do.
   c. You tell the peer you have the same problem; offer to go along to a meeting or professional consultation.
   d. You advise the person how to access help but do not disclose your own issue.

9. A friend reveals a suicide plan and swears you to secrecy.
   a. You keep a secret; that's what friends do.
   b. You say you are going to tell a teacher, counselor or parent unless he/she calls the suicide hotline immediately.
   c. You tell a trusted adult immediately and/or call 911 or your local emergency services number.
   d. You tell the person you will go along with him to tell a parent, trusted adult or to an emergency room.

10. You are becoming addicted to online games or sites you are not supposed to view.
    a. You continue and say to yourself, *Who does it hurt?*
    b. You decide to limit it to one hour daily.
    c. You tell your parents and ask them to monitor your computer use.
    d. You talk with a school counselor about why you do this and better ways to meet your needs.

TEENS – Body Image and Beyond

Pro and Con

FOR THE FACILITATOR

I. Purpose
To contemplate character traits in action and to consider outcomes from behavioral choices.

II. General Comments
The scenarios address qualities like integrity, loyalty, assertion, humility, honesty, responsibility, ethics, prioritizing, service to others, judgment, etc.

III. Possible Activities

1. **Individual Activity First**
   a. Ask a volunteer to place palms up; a peer puts a book in one hand and a pen in the other.
   b. Ask *Which is heavier?*
   c. Explain that decisions are made by thinking about outcomes and weighing pros and cons.
   d. Distribute *Pro and Con* handout; tell teens NOT to decide whether responses are right or wrong.
   e. Teens read each number silently and privately circle the letter indicating what they would do.
   f. They need not reveal their responses.
   g. Then, teens take turns reading each scenario aloud and giving a pro and con for each option, or play the game (below).

2. **Team Game**
   a. A volunteer who is comfortable reading aloud plays game show host.
   b. A scorekeeper to tallies each team's points, (up to 18), and records each team's winning rounds.
   c. Teams select a category and number, i.e. *Dating #2* or *Friends #6*; they win 2 or 6 points until they reach 18 which is a win for that round.
   d. Divide the group into two teams, team mates sit close enough to each other to collaborate.
   e. The goal is not to decide which options are best or worst but to consider outcomes for each.
   f. Team members take turns selecting a category and number (1-10) and accrue that number of points by stating a positive and negative consequence for each option a-d.
   g. Example: a team might pick "Problems, #9" on one turn, "Friends, #8" the next turn, and "Dating, #1" the next turn to accrue 18 points and win a round.
   h. Any combination of numbers to equal but not exceed 18 wins a round.
   i. As numbers are completed, the host crosses them out.
   j. When a team gets 18 points and wins the round, the game continues with the remaining numbers.
   k. When no combinations are left to equal 18, teams keep playing to accrue points; the team winning the most rounds and/or the most additional points is the winner.

IV. Enrichment Activities
   a. Teams develop their own scenarios for *Pro and Con* (with options) or for *What Would You Do?* (teens respond with their own ideas, no options listed), and read them to the opposing team.
   b. Encourage discussion and debate about topics teens see as particularly controversial.
   c. Play the *Pro and Con* Team Game as *What Would You Do?*
   - Teens put away their handouts; list topics on the board.
   - Teams select topics and numbers.
   - Game show host reads the scenarios (without options a-d).
   - Teens share what they would do, which may be different than any of the choices on the handout.
   - They accrue points and win as noted in the Team Game description.

Beyond Body

Self-Centered or Not in Vain?

If I Can Stop One Heart from Breaking

If I can stop one heart from breaking,
I shall not live in vain;
If I can ease one life the aching,
Or cool one pain,
Or help one fainting robin
Unto his nest again,
I shall not live in vain.

~ Emily Dickenson

1. To be vain is to be self-centered; on whom does the author focus?
   _____
   _____

2. Whose heart, life and/or pain might you lift, and how?
   _____
   _____

3. Who is your fainting robin?
   _____
   _____

4. How might you help your fainting robin unto the nest again?
   _____
   _____

5. To live in vain means one's life is useless; how will you make your life count?
   _____
   _____

TEENS – Body Image and Beyond

Self-Centered or Not in Vain?

FOR THE FACILITATOR

I. Purpose
To find purpose and worth in helping others.

II. General Comments
Teens may be pursuing and prioritizing good looks, popularity, and accolades for scholastic, athletic, or other achievements. The poem helps them see compassionate action as (perhaps the highest?) reason for living.

III. Possible Activities
a. Ideally, ask a volunteer to kneel down and look into a mirror on the floor, or to draw a person bending over water.
b. Ask teens to recall the mythological Narcissus (who was obsessed with his own reflection and eventually fell into the water and drowned).
c. Ask what it means to be *vain*; (self-absorbed, narcissistic).
d. Ask what it means if you study in vain for a test; (get a low grade despite your efforts).
e. Distribute the *Self-Centered or Not in Vain* handout.
f. Ask a volunteer to read the poem aloud.
g. Allow time to complete Numbers 1-5.
h. Remind teens to use code names when referring to actual people.
i. Encourage teens to share their responses.

IV. Enrichment Activities
a. Ask teens to brainstorm breaking hearts, aching lives, pain, and fainting robins.
b. A volunteer lists their ideas on the board. Possibilities:

Broken Hearts	Aching Lives	Pain	Fainting Robins
People who experience a break-up or suffer a loss of a loved one; those who feel rejected or lonely; people who have been betrayed or who condemn themselves for wrongdoing.	People who live in poverty or oppression; people in abusive relationships; those harboring hate and resentment; people obsessed with the past or fearing the future.	People who experience mental or physical illness or injury; victims of bullying or those who lash out in anger because of their own emotional anguish.	Frail children or the elderly; people who face debilitation and death; those who struggle with addictions and relapse; people who fall from positions of prestige or persevere in an uphill battle.

c. Ask teens ways they might help others and not live in vain. Possibilities:
- Volunteer at foods banks, hospitals, homeless shelters, animal rescues, etc.
- Work with charitable organizations to help disaster victims or the needy.
- Use talents in writing, art, music, drama, comedy, to reach people emotionally or through humor.
- Use intellect to tutor younger students or peers.
- Use personal experiences or knowledge for the greater good: speak to youth about dangers of texting while driving, drinking and drugs, gang violence, bullying, etc.
- Participate in support groups for teens whose parents have addiction issues, who have chemical dependency themselves, who struggle with eating disorders or other problems.

Beyond Body

Never Say Never

Compensation

Who never wept, knows laughter but a jest;
Who never failed, no victory has sought;
Who never suffered, never lived his best;
Who never doubted, never really thought;
Who never feared, real courage has not shown;
Who never faltered, lacks a real intent;
Whose soul was never troubled has not known
The sweetness and the peace of real content.
  ~ E. M. Brainard

Failure is part of my victory regarding …

_____
_____
_____
_____

I show courage in the face of fear when I …

_____
_____
_____
_____

Despite stumbling, I keep trying to …

_____
_____
_____
_____

My troubles teach me this about contentment …

_____
_____
_____
_____

TEENS – Body Image and Beyond

Never Say Never

FOR THE FACILITATOR

I. Purpose
To acknowledge ways that adversity is part of achievement.

To recognize how perceived weaknesses are stepping stones to strengths.

II. General Comments
Teens (and adults) dislike seemingly negative experiences and negative emotions (sadness, failure, suffering, doubt, fear, faltering, and trouble). The poem explains how these are precursors to positive experiences and emotions, (laughter, victory, life at its best, critical thinking, courage, strong intent, peace and contentment).

III. Possible Activities
   a. Ask a volunteer to draw two ice skaters on the board, facing each other, pushing each other, hands on hands.
   b. Ask teens what will happen as the two skaters push each other?
      Example: *They both move away from each other, equal distances.*
   c. Ask them to recall Newton's third law of motion.
      Example: *For every action there is an equal and opposite reaction.*
   d. Explain that experiences and emotions can be equal and opposite which works in our favor.
   e. Distribute the *Never Say Never* handout.
   f. Ask a volunteer to read the poem aloud.
   g. Allow time to complete the sentence starters in writing.
   h. Encourage teens to share their responses.

IV. Enrichment Activities
   a. Ask teens to apply to their lives other concepts in the poem:
      - Who never wept, knows laughter but a jest.
      - Who never suffered, never lived his best.
      - Who never doubted, never really thought.
   b. Ask teens to brainstorm other seemingly negative experiences and emotions that lead to or amplify positive experiences and emotions.

      Possibilities:
      - Who never knew anger, never extended a hand to forgive.
      - Who never erred, never felt the gift of mercy.
      - Who never experienced lack or poverty, never appreciated abundance or prosperity.
      - Who never struggled to learn a subject, was never sufficiently challenged.
      - Who was never tempted to give up, never proved perseverance.
   c. Ask teens to share experiences wherein negatives resulted in positives in their lives.
   d. Ask teens to share current challenges and the strengths they are developing.

Beyond Body

SILENT HEROES

In December 2012 a gunman forced his way into Sandy Hook Elementary School in Connecticut. He killed 26 people, mostly children ages six and seven.

Examples of heroism included a teacher shielding the children, a principal and a school psychologist confronting the gunman, as well as three other brave teachers who all lost their lives. Other children in the school were kept as calm as possible and their lives were saved by other brave staff who were able to move them out of harm's way, and through additional efforts.

In honor of all of the people involved at Sandy Hook, you can make your world a better place through random acts of kindness. Examples include wiping up a spill to prevent someone's fall, a smile and a kind word to lift a stranger's mood, helping someone in need to cross the street, etc.

Carry out a random act of kindness, with no expectation of reward, safe in the knowledge that one day someone might do the same for you.

~ Princess Diana

Share a time when your compassion helped someone.

_____

_____

Share a time when someone's thoughtfulness benefitted you.

_____

_____

Will you make a commitment to honor the Silent Heroes of the Sandy Hook Elementary School tragedy? Sign below to perform one act of kindness today and each day for a week. Note your acts of kindness each day. (It may even become a habit)

I will perform one act of kindness today and every day this week in honor of the Silent Heroes.

_____
Signature and Date

1) _____
2) _____
3) _____
4) _____
5) _____
6) _____
7) _____

TEENS – Body Image and Beyond

SILENT HEROES

FOR THE FACILITATOR

I. Purpose

To recognize that decency exists amidst horrific circumstances.

To motivate teens to become *silent heroes* in their spheres of influence through random acts of kindness.

II. General Comments

The Sandy Hook tragedy and other disasters provide opportunities to commemorate victims. Teens note that strength often develops through adversity and compassion.

III. Possible Activities

a. Encourage a discussion about heroes emerging during crises.

b. Describe the following scenario:
- A boy was bullied because of thick glasses.
- One day the glasses fell and a peer retrieved and returned the glasses with a smile and brief conversation.
- The boy with the glasses had planned to harm himself, but changed his mind due to the peer's kindness.

c. Encourage teens to identify the hero, what he did, and how a seemingly small act saved a life.

d. Distribute *Silent Heroes* handout; teens take turns reading aloud the informational lines.

e. Allow time for completion of the two questions.

f. Encourage teens to share their responses.

g. Ask teens to pledge to perform and document one random act of kindness daily for a week.

h. After a week, ask teens to discuss how their lives may have changed by benefitting others.

IV. Enrichment Activities

1. Ask teens to brainstorm ways they might, as a group, lighten people's burdens.

    Examples:
    - Making inspirational cards and sending them to nursing home residents.
    - Singing, playing musical instruments or performing cheerleading for children in hospitals.

2. Read the *Levels of Charity* written by Maimonides, 12th century scholar and physician.

    They are all acts of charity! They are rated from the lowest level to the highest level.

    1. Giving begrudgingly
    2. Giving less that you should, but giving it cheerfully
    3. Giving after being asked
    4. Giving before being asked
    5. Giving when you do not know the recipient's identity, but the recipient knows your identity
    6. Giving when you know the recipient's identity, but the recipient doesn't know your identity
    7. Giving when neither party knows the other's identity
    8. Enabling the recipient to become self-reliant

Internet Resources

At the time of this printing the websites and telephone numbers are current. We apologize if they change and suggest researching the subject online with reliable websites.

About.com Teen Health, Body Image and other topics www.about.com

Australian Youth Forum www.youth.gov.au/bodyimage

Centers for Disease Control, Lesbian, Gay, Bisexual and Transgender, LGBT, www.cdc.gov/lgbthealth/youth

CNN Heroes, CNN Health, www.cnn.com/SPECIALS/cnn.heroes; www.cnn.com/HEALTH/index

Drug EnforcementAgency, DEA.gov, www.justice.gov/dea/prevention

DEA resources www.GetSmartAboutDrugs.com, for teens www.JustThinkTwice.com

Dove Campaign for Real Beauty www.dove.us/Social-Mission/campaignforrealbeauty

Johns Hopkins Bloomberg School of Public Health Center for Adolescent Health www.jhsph.edu

Kids Health for food, fitness, body image, www.kidshealth.org/teen

Lets Move, www.letsmove.gov

Los Angeles and Southern California KABC Kool Kids, www.abclocal.go.com/kabc

Mayo Clinic, www.mayoclinic.com

My Plate, from U.S. Department of Agriculture, www.choosemyplate.gov

National Council of Youth Sports, www.youthsports@ncys.org

National Eating Disorder Association, www.nationaleatingdisorder.org NEDA Helpline 800-931-2237

National Institute on Drug Abuse NIDA, (steroids), www.teensdrugabuse.gov

National Institute of Mental Health, NIMH, www.nimh.nih.gov

National Suicide Prevention Lifeline, www.suicidepreventionlifeline.org 1-800-273-TALK (8255)

ObamaFoodarama web blog, www.obamafoodarama.blogspot.com

Overeaters Anonymous, www.oa.org

Self Abuse Finally Ends, S.A.F.E., www.safe-alternatives.com 1-800-DONTCUT (366-8288)

Substance Abuse and Mental Health Services Administration, SAMHSA, www.samhsa.gov

Teen Health website from The Nemours Foundation, www.kidshealth.org/teens

WebMD Teen Health Center www.teen.webmd.com

Whole Person Associates is the leading publisher of training resources for professionals who empower people to create and maintain healthy lifestyles. Our creative resources will help you work effectively with your clients in the areas of stress management, wellness promotion, mental health and life skills.

Please visit us at our web site: **www.wholeperson.com**. You can check out our entire line of products, place an order, request our print catalog, and sign up for our monthly special notifications.

Whole Person Associates

800-247-6789